Communications
in Computer and Information Science   102

Vinu V Das   Janahanlal Stephen   Nessy Thankachan
Srinivasa K. G.   Hatim A. Aboalsamh
Mohammad Hammoudeh   Vahid Salmani
Dinesh Kumar Tyagi   Anjali Mohapatra
Bharatheesh Jaysimha   Eliathamby Ambikairajah
Jon Blackledge (Eds.)

Power Electronics and Instrumentation Engineering

International Conference, PEIE 2010
Kochi, Kerala, India, September 7-9, 2010
Proceedings

 Springer

Main Editors

Vinu V Das
Engineers Network, Trivandrum, Kerala, India
E-mail: vinuvdas@gmail.com

Janahanlal Stephen
Mangalam College of Engineering, Ettumanoor
Kottayam, India
E-mail: drlalps@gmail.com

Nessy Thankachan
College of Engineering, Trivandrum, Kerala, India
E-mail: nessythankachan@gmail.com

Library of Congress Control Number: 2010934003

CR Subject Classification (1998): D.2, I.4, C.3, B.6, C.5.3, C.5.4

ISSN   1865-0929
ISBN-10   3-642-15738-6 Springer Berlin Heidelberg New York
ISBN-13   978-3-642-15738-7 Springer Berlin Heidelberg New York

springer.com

© Springer-Verlag Berlin Heidelberg 2010
Printed in Germany

Typesetting: Camera-ready by author, data conversion by Scientific Publishing Services, Chennai, India
Printed on acid-free paper   06/3180   5 4 3 2 1 0

Volume Editors

Preface

This book contains the best papers of the International Conference on Advances in Power Electronics and Instrumentation Engineering, PEIE 2010, organized by the Association of Computer Electronics and Electrical Engineers (ACEEE), during September 7–9, 2010 in Kochi, Kerala, India.

PEIE is an international conference integrating two major areas of electrical engineering – power electronics and instrumentation. Thus this conference reflects a continuing effort to increase the dissemination of recent research results among professionals who work in the areas of power electronics, instrumentation and electrical engineering

The program of this joint conference included several outstanding keynote lectures presented by internationally renowned distinguished researchers who are experts in the various PEIE areas. Their keynote speeches have contributed to heightening the overall quality of the program and significance of the theme of the conference.

I hope that you will find this collection of the best PEIE 2010 papers an excellent source of inspiration as well as a helpful reference for research in the aforementioned areas.

Organizing a conference like this one is not possible without the assistance and continuous support of many people and institutions. I thank Stefan Goeller, Janahanlal Stephen, R Vijay Kumar, and Nessy Thankachan for their constant support and guidance. I would like to express my gratitude to Springer's LNCS-CCIS editorial team, especially Leonie Kunz, for producing such a wonderful proceedings book.

July 2010   Vinu V Das

PEIE 2010 – Organization

Technical Chair

Hicham Elzabadani   American University in Dubai, UAE
Prafulla Kumar Behera Utkal University, India

Technical Co-chair

Natarajan Meghanathan Jackson State University, USA
Gylson Thomas   MES College of Engineering, India

General Chair

Janahanlal Stephen   VJCET, India
Beno Benhabib   University of Toronto, Canada

Publication Chair

R Vijaykumar   NSS CE, Palakkadu, India
Brajesh Kumar Kaoushik IIT Roorke, India

Organizing Chair

Vinu V Das   Engineers Network, India
Nessy T   Electrical Machines Group, ACEEE

Program Committee Chair

Harry E. Ruda   University of Toronto, Canada
Durga Prasad Mohapatra NIT Rourkela, India

Program Committee Members

Shu-Ching Chen   Florida International University, USA
T.S.B. Sudarshan   BITS Pilani, India
Habibollah Haro   Technological University of Malaysia
Derek Molloy   Dublin City University, Ireland
Jagadeesh Pujari   SDM College of Engineering and Technology,
         India
Nupur Giri   VESIT, Mumbai, India

Animesh Adhikari	S P Chowgule College, India
Anirban Mukhopadhyay	University of Kalyani, India
Malabika Basu	Dublin Institute of Technology, Ireland
Tahseen Al-Doori	American University in Dubai, UAE
V.K. Bhat	SMVD University, India
Ranjit Abraham	Armia Systems, India
Naomie Salim	Technological University of Malaysia
Abdullah Ibrahim	University of Malaysia, Pahang, Malaysia
Charles McCorkell	Dublin City University, Ireland
Neeraj Nehra	SMVD University, India
Muhammad Nubli	University of Malaysia Pahang, Malaysia
Zhenyu Y Angz	Florida International University, USA
Keivan Navi	Shahid Beheshti University, Iran
Rama Shankar Yadav	MNNIT, India
Smriti Agrawal	MNNIT, India
Vandana Bhattacherjee	BITS Mesra, India
R.D. Sudhaker Samuel	S J College of Engineering, India
Amitabha Sinha	West Bengal University of Technology, India
Shyam Lal	Mit Moradabad, India
Debasish Jena	Biju Patnaik University of Technology, India
Srinivasa K G	M S Ramaiah Institute of Technology, India
Bipin Bihari Jayasingh	CVR College of Engineering, India
Seyed-Hassan Mirian-Hosseinabadi	Sharif University of Technology, Iran
Malay K. Pakhira	Kalyani Government Engineering College, India
Sarmistha Neogy	Jadavpur University, India
Sreenath Niladhuri	Podicherry Engineering College, India
Ananta Ojha	ICFAI University, India
A K Sharma	YMCA Institute of Engineering, India
Debasis Giri	IIT Kharagpur, India
Suparna Biswas	WBUT, India

Table of Contents

Full Paper

PEIE 2010 - Short Paper

PEIE 2010 - Poster Paper

Novel Design for RF MEMS Capacitive Shunt Switch in K and Ku Bands

Rakesh S. Lal, A. Amalin Prince, and Iven Jose

Department of Electrical & Electronics Engineering
BITS, Pilani – K. K. Birla Goa Campus
Zuarinagar, Goa, India
rakeshslal1989@gmail.com, amalinprince@gmail.com,
iven@bits-goa.ac.in

Abstract. A novel design for RF MEMS Capacitive Shunt Switch with operating bandwidth in the K and Ku bands is presented in this paper. The novel MEMS switch has got lower insertion loss than a normal switch and there is no compromise on the isolation and the operating bandwidth of the switch. The resonant frequency of the proposed switch is kept constant near 20GHz which is the midpoint of the bandwidth of the switch. A comparative study of a normal switch and the proposed switch is done. The improvement in design has been achieved by introducing discontinuities in the coplanar waveguide both in the central conductor and the ground planes. The discontinuities are represented in terms of equivalent lumped parameters. A new method of obtaining the lumped parameters of coplanar waveguide step discontinuities in the central conductor and ground planes using full wave electromagnetic simulation is also presented.

Keywords: MEMS, RF MEMS, Capacitive shunt switch, CPW, SAW shaped CPW, Lumped Parameter.

1 Introduction

Radio Frequency Microelectromechanical Systems (RF MEMS) is gaining popularity day by day as is obvious from the vast amount of research done on this field. The field finds vast applications in space and telecommunication. Till date the most important and most researched device in RF MEMS is the switch. In comparison to contemporary state-of-the-art switching devices, MEMS switches exhibit superior electrical performance and low power consumption on a size commensurate with that of the solid state devices [1]. RF MEMS switches exhibit improvement in performance figure-of-merit and losses over conventional switches in orders of magnitude. The inevitable I-V non-linearities associated with semiconductor junctions in PIN diodes and GaAs FETs are non-existent, except for the minor hysteresis in C-V characteristics of shunt switches [1].

Capacitive shunt switches are preferred over series switches in the K and Ku bands due to their higher power handling capability [2]. Improvement in design of capacitive shunt switch was done by Wu, Q. et al. by introducing step discontinuity in the

V. V Das, J. Stephen, and N. Thankachan et al. (Eds.): PEIE 2010, CCIS 102, pp. 1–9, 2010.

central conductor of the CPW, resulting in better return loss and insertion loss of the switch [3]. Implementation of Distributed MEMS Transmission Line (DMTL) phase shifters using such a CPW has also been demonstrated [3-6]. But the associated disadvantage with this CPW is that the operating frequency of the switch shifts to higher values which is not desirable. The resonant frequency of the switch increases and hence the average isolation in the K and Ku bands becomes poorer than the corresponding value for the normal CPW. Hence a design is required which does not affect the frequency range of the switch and at the same time provides good average insertion loss and isolation similar to that of the SAW shaped CPW [3]. This is achieved in the switch is presented in this paper.

This paper is organized as follows. Section 2 explains the working mechanism of a Capacitive shunt switch. Section3 presents the performance comparison of the new switch with an existing capacitive shunt switch to stress upon the advantages of the new switch. Section 4 explains the extraction of lumped parameter model to model electrically the working of the proposed switch. Section 5 explains the results and finally Section 6 provides some conclusions.

2   Capacitive Shunt Switch

A MEMS capacitive shunt switch on CPW configuration is shown in Fig. 1. The two ends of the MEMS bridge are fixed on the ground planes of the CPW and the bridge is suspended over the transmission line.

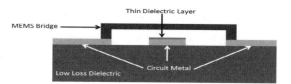

Fig. 1. Capacitive shunt switch implemented on CPW

When the MEMS bridge is suspended above the transmission line the signal passes through without any attenuation, under ideal conditions. The switch is operated by applying a DC voltage between the bridge and the transmission line. This results in an electrostatic force between the bridge and the transmission line, causing the bridge to bend down and touch the dielectric layer on the transmission line. This results in a short circuit between the transmission line and the ground planes hence causing the RF signal to be shunted to the ground planes and hence a reflective switch results. The voltage reflection coefficient is calculated using (1).

$$\tau^2 = \frac{Z_L - Z_o}{Z_L + Z_o} \tag{1}$$

Where, Z_L = impedance of switch, Z_o = characteristic impedance of line reflection loss parameter,

$$S11 = 10\log\tau^2 \quad \text{dB} \tag{2}$$

transmission loss parameter, $\quad S_{12} = 10\log T^2 \quad \text{dB} \tag{3}$

where, $\qquad\qquad\qquad T^2 = 1 - \tau^2 \tag{4}$

The S_{12} in the ON state and OFF state of the switch is referred to as insertion loss and isolation respectively. The isolation is maximum at a particular frequency called the resonant frequency of the switch. It is given by the formula

$$f = \frac{1}{2\pi\sqrt{LC}} \quad \text{Hz} \tag{5}$$

When the DC voltage is removed, the bridge springs back to the normal position and the RF signal passes through.

3 Normal CPW Configuration

A normal CPW is shown in Fig. 2. The simulation results using Ansoft HFSS are presented.

3.1 ON State

The simulation plots of the ON state scattering parameters are shown in Fig. 3 and Fig.4. The insertion losses at 12GHz, 20GHz and 27GHz are -0.18dB, -0.48dB and -0.84dB respectively. The average insertion loss in K and Ku bands combined is -0.48dB.

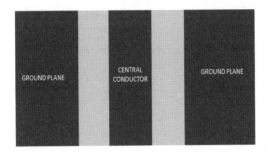

Fig. 2. Normal CPW (top view)

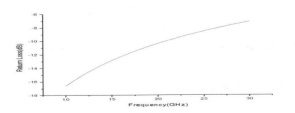

Fig. 3. Variation of ON state return loss with frequency for normal CPW

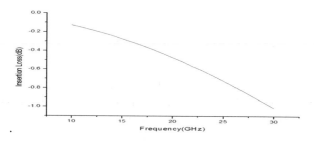

Fig. 4. Variation of insertion loss with frequency for normal CPW

The simulation plots of the OFF state scattering parameters are shown in Fig. 5 and Fig.6. The resonant frequency is 21GHz, which is almost the mid pint of the operating frequency range, that is Ku and K bands combined. As a result, the switch by default has got good isolation, that is, isolation greater than 20dB in magnitude throughout the Ku and K bands.

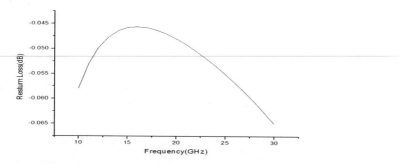

Fig. 5. Variation of OFF state return loss with frequency for normal CPW

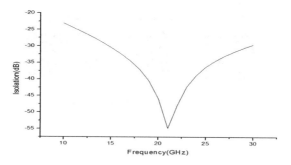

Fig. 6. Variation of isolation with frequency for normal CPW

4 New CPW Configuration

A novel CPW configuration enhancing the operating characteristics of RF MEMS Capacitive shunt switch is shown in Fig. 7. Here step discontinuities are introduced in the transmission line as well as the ground planes.

4.1 ON State

The simulation plots of the ON state scattering parameters are shown in Fig. 8 and Fig. 9. The insertion losses at 12GHz, 20GHz and 27GHz are -0.12dB, -0.25dB and -0.43dB respectively. All these values are considerably less than the corresponding values for normal CPW. The average insertion loss in the Ku and K bands combined is -0.25dB. This value is almost half the value of the normal CPW average insertion loss.

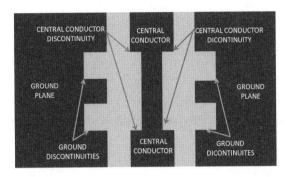

Fig. 7. CPW with central conductor and ground plane discontinuities(top view)

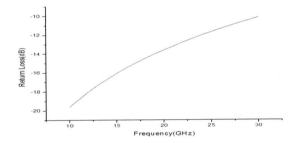

Fig. 8. Variation of ON state return loss with frequency for new CPW

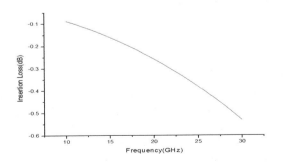

Fig. 9. Variation of insertion loss with frequency for new CPW

4.2 OFF State

The simulation plots of the OFF state scattering parameters are shown in Fig. 10 and Fig. 11. From the isolation versus frequency plot it is clear that the resonant frequency is 21GHz which is the same as that of the normal switch. Also throughout the operating frequency of the switch the isolation is greater than 20dB. Hence there is no compromise on the isolation of the switch in case of the new CPW configuration.

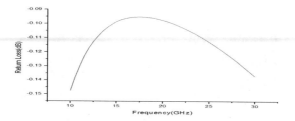

Fig. 10. Variation of OFF state return loss with frequency for new CPW

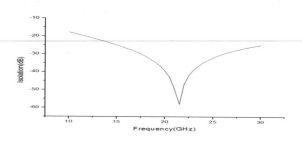

Fig. 11. Variation of isolation with frequency for new CPW

5 Extraction of Lumped Parameter Model

An equivalent lumped parameter modeling is done for the new CPW. The new modeling is done by analyzing the resonant frequency of the switch. The capacitance of the switch in OFF state is calculated using (5).

$$C = \frac{\varepsilon_o \varepsilon_r A}{t_d} \qquad (6)$$

ε_o = permittivity of vacuum, ε_r = relative permittivity of dielectric layer, A = area of overlap of switch with the transmission line, t_d = thickness of dielectric layer.

The capacitance is calculated to be 6.4pF using (6). Substituting the capacitance value in (5) the inductance is calculated to be 9.3pH.The step discontinuity in the central conductor of a CPW has been analyzed by various authors and different models have been proposed [7-9]. The different models have been tested using software simulations. The softwares used are Ansoft HFSS and Agilent ADS. Finally an equivalent circuit model consistent with the simulation results is proposed.

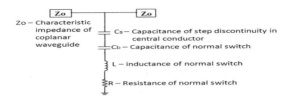

Fig. 12. Lumped Parameter model of CPW with step discontinuity in the central conductor

Simulation results of a switch implemented on a CPW with step discontinuity in central conductor, which have not been included in this paper due to space constraints, show an increase in resonant frequency of the switch to 27GHz. The increase in resonant frequency coupled with the insertion loss decrease, indicate that a new capacitance has been introduced in series with shunt impedance branch representing the switch. The added capacitance value is calculated using (1) and turns out to be 9.15pF. The lumped parameter of the switch along with the step discontinuity in central conductor is shown in Fig. 12.To confirm the validity of the equivalent model, the lumped parameter model simulation was done with Agilent ADS. The plot matches with the simulation results from HFSS hence confirming the assumption.

The equivalent lumped model for the ground plane discontinuities is analyzed using the same technique as presented in the above case of step discontinuity in central conductor. The capacitance of the switch is calculated using (6) and the value is 18.0pF. It is observed that the resonant frequency gets shifted to 15 GHz. The resonant frequency decrease along with the insertion loss decrease, as compared to a normal switch with resonant frequency of 21GHz, indicate that a new inductance has been introduced in series with the shunt impedance branch of the switch. The added inductance value is calculated using (5) and turns out to be 6.25pH. The lumped parameter of the switch in OFF state along with the ground discontinuity is shown in Fig. 13.

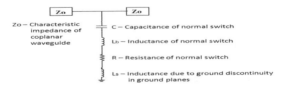

Fig. 13. Lumped Parameter model of CPW with step discontinuity in the ground planes

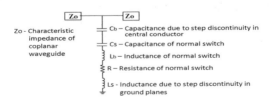

Fig. 14. Lumped Parameter of the novel switch with discontinuities in central conductor and ground planes

To confirm the validity of the equivalent circuit model , the lumped parameter model simulation was done with Agilent ADS. The plot matches with the simulation results from HFSS. The insertion loss plot of the OFF state of the switch also matches with the corresponding plot from HFSS. Hence the lumped model of the ground discontinuity shown in Fig. 13 is proved to be valid. Finally the lumped model of the CPW configuration shown in Fig. 7 is obtained as shown in Fig. 14 combining the two derived models. The isolation plot is shown in Fig. 15. It matches with the plot from HFSS shown in Fig. 11. Based on the above observations a new method is identified for extracting the equivalent circuit model for CPW step discontinuities. Step discontinuities on CPWs are of 2 types: 1) discontinuities on the central conductor, 2) discontinuities on the ground plane. As proved earlier in the case of the new CPW configuration, the discontinuities on the central conductor result in a shunt capacitance in the equivalent circuit model and discontinuities on the ground plane results in shunt inductance in the equivalent circuit model.

Based on these ideas a generalized method for extracting the equivalent circuit model of any CPW step discontinuity using full wave electromagnetic simulation is presented. Construct a MEMS capacitive shunt switch type bridge over the portion of the CPW where step discontinuities are present. The length and breadth of the switch should be such that it covers the entire region where the discontinuities are present. A dielectric layer should be placed over the central conductor and should be of the exact shape as that of the discontinuity on the central conductor. The bridge should touch the dielectric layer on the central conductor. The capacitance can be easily computed using (6).

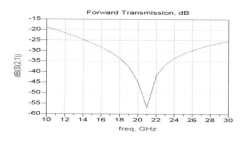

Fig. 15. Variation of isolation with frequency for new CPW obtained from Agilent ADS

The next step is to simulate the structure on Ansoft HFSS. Extract the S_{12} parameter for a range of frequencies till the first minima is obtained. Perform simulation starting from 1GHz till a minima is found. The frequency corresponding to the minima is the resonant frequency. Substitute the value of frequency obtained from simulation and the calculated value of capacitance from (6) into (5) and obtain the value of inductance. Hence the net shunt capacitances and inductances can be determined. This method is valid for step discontinuities on both the central conductor and the ground planes of CPW.

6   Results

The return loss and insertion loss for the proposed switch is found to be better in comparison to the conventional switch. The average insertion loss for normal switch is calculated to be -0.48dB whereas for the proposed switch the value is -0.25dB, hence making a large improvement in the performance of the switch in the K and Ku bands. Moreover there is no compromise on the isolation. A unique technique to obtain the lumped parameter model without involving rigorous mathematical calculations is also presented.

7 Conclusion

A novel RF MEMS capacitive shunt switch is developed for telecommunications applications. The proposed switch will find enormous application in RF MEMS phase shifters where switches with low insertion losses are required. The new method presented to obtain lumped parameter model of CPW step discontinuities can enable quick and easy analysis of CPW based devices.

References

1. Rangra, K.J.: Electrostatic Low Actuation Voltage RF-MEMS Switches for Telecommunications. Ph.D. Dissertation, Dept. of Information and Communication Technology, University of Trento, Italy (February 2005)
2. Rebeiz, G.M.: RF MEMS theory, design and technique. John Wiley & Sons Inc., Hoboken (2003)
3. Wu, Q., Tang, K., Feng, Z.-R., Sun, F.-L., Li, L.-W.: DMTL Phase Shifter using Insulation Layer and SAW shaped CPW. In: IEEE Asia Pacific Microwave Conference (2007)
4. Barker, N.S., Rebeiz, G.M.: Optimization of Distributed MEMS Phase Shifters. In: IEEE MTT-S International Microwave Symposium Digest, vol. 1, pp. 3–19 (June 1999)
5. Dey, S., Rangra, K.J., Shrivastava, S.J.: Design Optimization of Low Loss Distributed RF MEMS Phase Shifter. In: International Conference of Mechanical and Electronics Engineering (ICMEE), Chennai, India (2009)
6. Borgioli, A., Liu, Y., Nagra, A.S., York, R.A.: Low loss Distributed MEMS Phase Shifter. IEEE Microwave and Guided wave letters 10(1) (January 2000)
7. Chiu, C.-W., Wu, R.-B.: Capacitance Computation for CPW Discontinuities with Finite Metallization Thickness by Hybrid Finite-Element Method. IEEE Trans. Microwave Theory Tech. 45(4), 498–504 (1997)
8. Chiu, C.-W.: Inductance Computation for Coplanar Waveguide Discontinuities with Finite Metallization Thickness. IEE Proc., Microwave Antennas Propag. 145(6), 496–500 (1998)
9. Sinclair, C., Nightingale, S.J.: An Equivalent Circuit Model for the Coplanar Waveguide Step Discontinuity. In: 1992 IEEE MTT-S International Microwave Symposium Digest, vol. 31-5, pp. 1461–1464 (June 1992)

Power System Dynamic Stability Enhancement of SMIB Using Fuzzy Logic Based Power System Stabilizer

Kamalesh Chandra Rout and P.C. Panda

Electrical Engineering Department, National Institute of Technology, Rourkela, India
rout.kamalesh@gmail.com

Abstract. The oscillations in the frequency range of 0.2 to 3.0 Hz limit the power transmission capability of a network and, sometimes, even cause a loss of synchronism and an eventual breakdown of the entire system. This paper presents an application of fuzzy logic power system stabilizer (PSS) for dynamic stability enhancement power system. Here speed deviation ($\Delta\omega$) and acceleration (ΔP) of the rotor synchronous generator were taken as the input to the fuzzy logic controller. Depending on these variables, the inference mechanism of the fuzzy logic controller is represented by a (7×7) decision table i.e. 49 if-then rules. The performance of the fuzzy PSS is compared with the conventional power system stabilizer (CPSS) and without PSS. The simulations were tested under different operating conditions.

Keywords: Power System Stabilizer, Dynamic Stability, SMIB, Fuzzy Sets and Logic.

1 Introduction

The electric power systems today are no longer operated as isolated systems, but as interconnected systems which may include thousands of electric elements and be spread over vast geographical areas. There are many advantages of interconnected power systems such as provide large amounts of power and increase reliability of the system, reduce the number of machines which are required for both operation at peak load, and required as spinning reserve to care of a sudden change of load. Stability of power system is one of the most important aspects in electric system operation. To enhance system damping, the generators are equipped with power system stabilizers (PSSs) that provide supplementary feedback stabilizing signals in the excitation systems. PSSs augment the power system stability limit and extend the power-transfer capability by enhancing the system damping of low-frequency oscillations associated with the electromechanical modes[1][2].

A System is said to be dynamically stable, if the oscillations do not acquire certain amplitude and die out quickly. Dynamic stability is concerned with small disturbances lasting for a long time. Conventional PSS (CPSS) is widely used in existing power systems and has made a contribution in enhancing power system dynamic stability. The parameters of CPSS are determined based on a linearised model of the power system around a nominal operating point where they can provide good performance. Since power systems are highly non-linear systems, with configurations and parameters that

V. V Das, J. Stephen, and N. Thankachan et al. (Eds.): PEIE 2010, CCIS 102, pp. 10–14, 2010.

change with time, the CPSS design based on the linearised model of the power system cannot guarantee its performance in a practical operating environment [3][4].

1.1 Power System Model

The nonlinear equations of the system are:

$$\frac{d\delta}{dt} = \omega_B S_m$$

$$\frac{dS_m}{dt} = \frac{1}{2H}[-DS_m + T_m - T_e]$$

$$\frac{dE_d'}{dt} = \frac{1}{T_{qo}'}[-E_d' + (x_q - x_q')i_q]$$

$$\frac{dE_q'}{dt} = \frac{1}{T_{do}'}[-E_q' + (x_d - x_d')i_d + E_{fd}]$$

$$\frac{dE_{fd}}{dt} = \frac{1}{T_a}[K_a(V_{ref} + V_s - V_t) - E_{fd}]$$

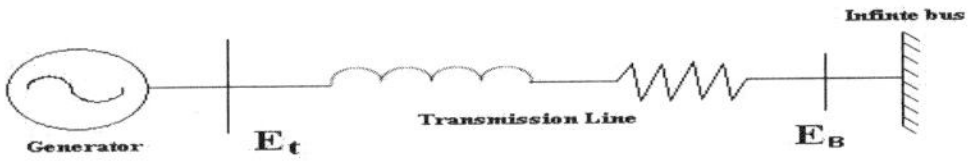

Fig. 1. Single Machine Infinite bus system

1.2 Excitation System Control Design

The specific objectives of excitation control design are:

- Maximization of the damping of the local plant mode as well as interarea mode oscillations without compromising the stability of other modes, such as the exciter mode.
- Enhancement of system transient stability.
- Prevention of adverse effects on system performance during major system upsets that cause large frequency and voltage excursions.
- Minimization of the consequences of excitation system malfunctions due to component failures.

With electric power systems, the change in electrical torque of a synchronous machine, following a small disturbance can be resolved into two components [5].

$$\Delta T_e = T_S \Delta\delta + T_D \Delta\omega$$

$T_S \Delta\delta$ is the component of torque change in phase with the rotor angle deviation $\Delta\delta$

$T_D \Delta\omega$ is the component of torque change in phase with the speed deviation $\Delta\omega$

T_S is the synchronizing torque coefficient

T_D is the damping torque coefficient

System stability depends on the existence of both components of torque.

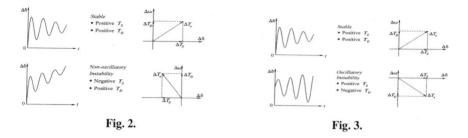

Fig. 2.   **Fig. 3.**

For a generator connected radially to a large power system, in the absence of automatic voltage regulator (i.e. with constant field voltage), the instability is due to the lack of sufficient synchronizing torque (i.e. $-ve$ T_S). This results in instability through a non-oscillatory mode as shown in Figure 2.

For a generator connected radially to a large power system, in the presence of automatic voltage regulator, the instability is due to the lack of sufficient damping torque (i.e. $-ve$ T_D). This results in instability through a oscillatory mode as shown in Figure 3.

1.3 PSS Structure

The phase compensation block provides the appropriate phase-lead characteristics to compensate for the phase-lag between the exciter input and the generator electrical torque [6]. Figure 4 shows a single 1st order block.

The signal washout block serves as a high pass filter, with the time constant T_w to allow signals associated with oscillations in w_r to pass unchanged. Without it, steady changes in speed would modify the terminal voltage. It allows the PSS to respond only to changes in speed.

The stabilizer gain K_{stab} determines the amount of damping introduces by the PSS.

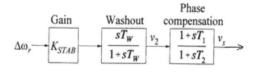

Fig. 4. PSS Structure

2 Fuzzy Logic Controller

The following Figure 5. Shows the block diagram of fuzzy logic controller.

Fig. 5. Block diagram of Fuzzy Logic Controller

In the design of fuzzy logic controllers, unlike most conventional methods, a mathematical model is not required to describe the system under study. Here control strategy depends upon a set of rules, which describes the behavior of the controller. It generally comprises four principle components: fuzzification interface, knowledge base, decision making logic and defuzzification interface. After choosing proper variables as input and output of fuzzy controller, it is required to decide on the linguistic variables. For the power system under study, seven linguistic variables for each of the input and output variables are used to describe them. The stabilizer output is obtained by applying a particular rule expressed in the form of membership function. Figure 6 shows the membership functions for input $\Delta\omega$ and ΔP and Figure 7 shows the membership function for output U. Decision table in 1 shows the result of 49 rules, where a positive control signal is for the deceleration control and a negative signal is for acceleration control.

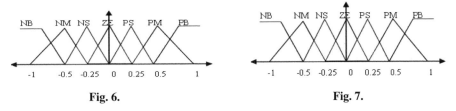

Fig. 6.   **Fig. 7.**

Table 1. Decision table of 49 rules

acc / speed dev.	NB	NM	NS	ZE	PS	PM	PB
NB	NB	NB	NB	NS	ZE	ZE	PS
NM	NB	NB	NM	NS	ZE	PS	PM
NS	NB	NB	NM	ZE	PS	PM	PB
ZE	NB	NM	NS	ZE	PS	PM	PB
PS	NB	NM	NS	ZE	PM	PB	PB
PM	NM	NS	ZE	PS	PM	PB	PB
PB	NS	ZE	ZE	PS	PB	PB	PB

3 Simulation Results

The test system depicted in Figure 1. is considered for analysis.

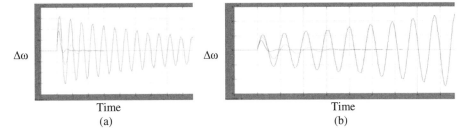

$\Delta\omega$ $\Delta\omega$

Time   Time
(a)   (b)

Fig. 8. Responses of generator when mechanical torque was changed into 0.1[pu] in 8(a) light load, 8(b) nominal load, 8(c) heavy load

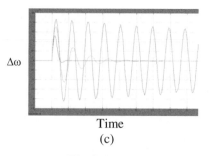

Time

(c)

Fig. 8. (*continued*)

4 Conclusion

The target of the developed work is the damping of oscillations related to power system using fuzzy logic controller based technique on a single machine to infinite bus system. The system without stabilizer is highly oscillatory. Both the controllers are able to damp the oscillations reasonably well or to stabilize the system at most of the operating conditions. From the simulation results FuzzyPSS shows the better control performance than CPSS and no PSS power system stabilizer in terms of settling time and damping effect.

References

1. Abido, M.A.: Hybridizing Rule - based Power System Stabilizers with Genetic Algorithms. IEEE Transactions on Power Systems 14, 600–607 (1999)
2. Voropai, N.I., Etingov, P.V.: Application of Fuzzy Logic Power System Stabilizers to Transient Stability Improvement in a Large Electric Power System. In: IEEE PowerCon 2002, pp. 1223–1227 (October 2002)
3. Kundur, P., Klein, M., Rogers, G.J., Zywno, M.S.: Application of Power System Stabilizers for Enhancement of Overall Stability, vol. 4, pp. 1463–1469 (May 1989)
4. Hosseinzadeh, N., Kalam, A.: A Rule-Based Fuzzy Power System Stabilizer Tuned by a Neural Network. IEEE Transactions on Energy Conversion 14(3) (1999)
5. Kundur, P.: Power System Control and Stability, pp. 3–168, 699–825, 1103–1166. McGraw-Hill, Inc., New York (1994)
6. Larsen, R.V., Swann, D.A.: Applying Power System Stabilizers, Part I, II, III. IEEE Transactions on PAS 100(6) (June 1981)

A Novel Configuration of Unified Power Flow Controller

S. Baskar[1], N. Kumarappan[2], and R. Gnanadass[3]

[1] Assistant Professor, Dept. of EEE, Sri Manakula Vinayagar Engineering College,
Puducherry, India
Tel.: +91 413 2244598, Mobile: 9443686695; Fax: +91 413 2641151
bas_good@hotmail.com
[2] Professor, Dept. of EEE, Annamalai University, India
kumarappan_n@yahoo.com
[3] Associate Professor, Dept. of EEE, Pondicherry Engineering College, India
gnanadass@yahoo.com

Abstract. This paper presents the modeling and design of Unified Power Flow Controller (UPFC) using novel control technique in the inverter. The proposed control technique implements the 150 degree conduction mode of individual IGBTs in the inverter. The UPFC can be operated using PWM controllers to enhance the reactive power compensating and regulating the line voltage and also reduces the harmonic in the transmission line current and voltage. The 150 degree inverter is advantageous and increases the RMS values of output voltages, when compared to 120° mode, and 180° mode. Total required VA rating of the inverters is reduced greatly over wide load conditions. The operating performance of UPFC is demonstrated on Single Machine Infinite Bus (SMIB) system for different case studies. The proposed model considerably improves the system stability by damping the oscillation during the vulnerable conditions.

Keywords: SMIB, Switching Level Modeling, 150 degree inverter, Unified Power Flow Controller.

1 Introduction

In recent years, new types of FACTS devices have been investigated that may be used to increase power system operation flexibility and controllability, to enhance system stability and to achieve better utilization of existing power systems. The evolution in power electronic devices along with the development and control have allowed the design and implementation of structural controllers known as Flexible AC Transmission System (FACTS), which are emerging as feasible technology for the improvement of system's dynamic behavior. The benefits arising from FACTS devices are widely appreciated. The concept of Flexible AC Transmission System (FACTS) was introduced [1,2] as a family of power electronic equipments which have emerged for controlling and optimizing flow of electrical power in the transmission line. The concepts of Unified Power Flow Controller (UPFC) its performance and steady state characteristics have been widely reported in the literature [3,4]. The UPFC has been researched broadly and many research articles dealing with UPFC modeling, analysis, control and application have been published in the recent

V. V Das, J. Stephen, and N. Thankachan et al. (Eds.): PEIE 2010, CCIS 102, pp. 15–19, 2010.
© Springer-Verlag Berlin Heidelberg 2010

years. Mathematical models were developed for UPFC to determine steady state operational characteristics using state space equations without considering the effects of converters and the dynamics of generator [5, 6]. The performance of UPFC was analyzed by designing a series converter using conventional and advanced controllers [7, 8]. Mathematical model of UPFC using general PWM and space vector approach was used to perform the power flow studies, Eigen analysis and transient stability investigations [9].A non linear dynamic small signal model of network with UPFC was established for transient studies. The model evaluated the compensation effects of UPFC, optimized the location of UPFC and its control design [10]. An equivalent two bus power network was developed based on sets of equations for a system including the UPFC was proposed. This provided a useful tool to rate; evaluate the performance of UPFC on power systems [11].

The UPFC was modeled as voltage source model and PWM switching level model. The voltage source model of UPFC was constructed with equivalent voltage source and impedances using MATLAB. The switching level model of UPFC was designed and simulated in EMTP.The equivalent impedance of voltage source model was found from the dynamic responses of UPFC switching level model. The results show that switching level model was more accurate than voltage source model [12]. The optimal location and equivalent impedance of UPFC are found by voltage source model and switching level model by varying the amplitude and phase angle of injected voltage [13].In laboratory implementation of FACTS devices, UPFC was setup by PWM modulation controllers which provides more effective control of real and reactive power flow [14].

The new configuration of UPFC has proposed. Two inverters are connected face to face on AC side instead of back to back through a common DC link. It greatly reduces the VA rating of the inverters [15].The new conduction mode of 120° inverter is implemented in the brushless DC motor and the performances are analyzed [16].The conduction mode of 150° implemented and it is analyzed for three phase inverter performance [17].The double band hysteresis current controller was designed for STATCOM to compensate the reactive power in the distribution network. The current error and switching frequency are reduced [18]. Hence in this paper, the proposed technique aims at to control the real and reactive power flow in the transmission lines, by implementing the 150° conduction angle for individual switches in the inverters.

In this paper dynamic control UPFC is analyzed with six pulse converter using switching level model. The architecture of the paper in Section 2 explains the conduction mode of inverter, section 3 describes the modeling of UPFC, and section 4 provides the simulation results. The conclusion is summarized in Section 5.

2   New Conduction Mode of Voltage Source Inverter (VSI)

In this 150° conduction mode of inverter topology twelve switching patterns are presented per cycle with each pattern duration is 30°. Three transistors conduct in one interval, while only two transistors conduct in the next one. The gating signals are shifted from each other by 60° to get three phase balanced voltages. A 30° dead-time period is provided between the firing of each two series-switches in each leg. The firing pulse waveform for IGBT as shown in Fig.1.

While comparing with 180° and 120° degree mode the advantage is to increases the RMS values of output voltages. It provides a 30° safety margin period, which is large enough, to avoid short circuit on the dc supply. It Produces seven level phase-voltage waveforms, $(0, \pm V_d/3, \pm V_d/2, \pm 2V_d/3)$, Compared to only four or three levels in 180° and 120° modes, respectively. It highly reduces the total harmonic distortion (THD) and DF of output voltage waveforms, by presenting 12-step waveforms, which are closer to the sinusoidal waveform compared to the original 6-step ones. The implementation of 150° inverter almost eliminates the low order harmonics that has 1/n of fundamental magnitude in previous mode, by improving the 1/n undesired magnitude relation.

Fig. 1. Firing pulse of 150° conduction mode

3 Modeling of UPFC

In SMIB model the synchronous generator is connected to the linear load through the Power transformer and " π "section model of transmission line. The UPFC is located at the middle of the transmission line. The shunt and series device of UPFC consists of three phase IGBT converter with PWM controller. The shunt converter is connected to the transmission line in parallel through a three phase transformer. The series converter is connected to the transmission line in series through the three single phase transformer.

This modeling is done with Simulink blockset and simulation is carried out in MATLAB environment as shown in Fig.2.

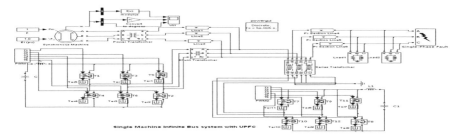

Fig. 2. Switching level model of Unified Power Flow Controller (UPFC)

4 Simulation Results

CASE (I)
In this case, the SMIB is connected with 75% and 125% base load condition. The real and reactive power tracings are obtained through simulation and their magnitudes

different load conditions are given in Fig.3 (a) & (b). After the insertion of UPFC, the power tracings are obtained with constant modulation index.

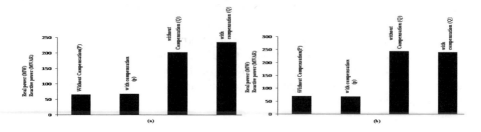

Fig. 3. Real and Reactive Power Flow before and after compensation (a) load 1 (b) load 2

CASE (II)

To illustrate the performance of UPFC in the transient conditions, a transmission single phase to ground fault is created at load end of the SMIB system. The fault is cleared at 0.1 seconds. The variation of line voltage and current before and after inserting the UPFC is obtained to illustrate its impact. The corresponding voltage and current wave forms are given in the Figures 4(a) & (b). The simulation results shows that after inserting the UPFC the voltage and current oscillations are very much reduced. It reaches its initial value quickly. The UPFC will produce stable state within half of the time in the fundamental frequency.

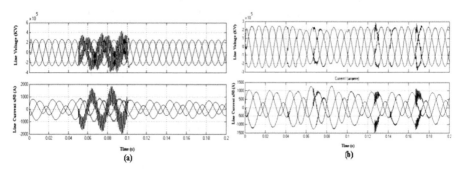

Fig. 4. Line voltage & line current during fault condition (a) before connecting UPFC (b) after connecting UPFC

5 Conclusion

In this paper, 150° conduction mode of three phase inverter is designed and implemented in Unified Power Flow Controller and the performance are analyzed. The simulation model is simulated using MATLAB/SIMULINK environment. These switching schemes have been implemented in the developed UPFC model & the performance is demonstrated on SMIB system with linear loads. This controller improves the performance of dynamic stability and transient stability and achieves good damping of power and voltage oscillations in the system.

References

[1] Hingorani, N.G.: Understanding FACTS-Concepts and Technology of Flexible AC Transmission Systems. In: IEEE Power Engineering society. Standard publishers, IEEE press (2001)

[2] Song, Y.H., Johns, A.T.: Flexible ac transmission systems FACTS. IEE, London (1999)

[3] Gyugi, L.: Unified Power-Flow Control Concept for Flexible AC Transmission Systems. Proceedings of IEE-C 139, 323–331 (1992)

[4] Gyugi, L., et al.: The Unified Power Flow Controller: A new approach to power transmission control. IEEE Trans. Power Delivery 10(2), 1085–1097 (1995)

[5] Papic, I.: Mathematical analysis of FACTS devices based on a voltage source converter, Part 1: mathematical models. Electric Power Systems Research 56, 139–148 (2000)

[6] Papic, I.: Mathematical analysis of FACTS devices based on a voltage source converter, Part II: steady state operational characteristics. Electric Power Systems Research 56, 149–157 (2000)

[7] Round, S.D., Yu, Q., Norum, L.E., Undeland, T.M.: Performance of a Unified power flow controller using A D-Q control system. In: AC and DC power transmission Conference Pub. No. 423. IEEE, Los Alamitos (1996)

[8] Yu, Q., Round, S.D., Norum, L.E., Undeland, T.M.: Dynamic control of UPFC, pp. 508–514. IEEE, Los Alamitos (1996)

[9] Nabavi-Niaki, A., Iravani, M.R.: Steady state dynamic model on UPFC. IEEE Trans. Power Systems 11(4) (1996)

[10] Smith, K.S., Ran, L., Penman, J.: Dynamic modeling of a unified power flow controller. IEE Proc. Gener. Transm. Distrib. 144(1) (1997)

[11] Keri, A.J.F., Lombard, X., Edris, A.A.: UPFC: Modeling and Analysis. IEEE Trans. on power Delivery 14(2) (1999)

[12] Won, D.-J., Chung, I., Moon, S.-I.: Determination of equivalent impedances of UPFC voltage-source model from the dynamic responses of UPFC switching-level model. Electric power systems 25, 463–470 (2003)

[13] Rajeswari, S., Gnanadass, R., Venkatesh, P.: Modeling of Unified power flow controller for active power Regulation. In: Institution of engineers, Calcutta, India, vol. 90, pp. 33–39 (2009)

[14] Dong, L., Crow, M.L., Yang, Z., Shen, C., Zhang, L., Atcitty, S.: A Reconfigurable FACTS system for University Laboratories. IEEE Trans. power systems 19(1), 120–128 (2004)

[15] Wang, J., Peng, F.Z.: A Novel Configuration of Unified Power Flow Controller. In: 18th IEEE power electronics Conference and exposition, vol. 2, pp. 919–924 (2003)

[16] Sudhoff, S.D., Krause, P.C.: Operating Modes of the Brushless DC Motor with a 120 Degree Inverter. IEEE transaction on Energy Conversion 5(3) (September 1990)

[17] Saied, M.H., Mostafa, M.Z., Abdel-Moneim, T.M., Yousef, H.A.: On Three Phase Six-Switches Voltage Source Inverter: A 150° Conduction Mode. Member IEEE, Alexandria Univercity (2006)

[18] Kim, B.S., Oh, W.H., Shin, E.C., Seo, S.J., Lee, S.B., Yoo, J.Y.: Current Control Method using a Double Band Hysteresis. In: IEEE conference, Busan, Korea (2004)

New Results on the Global Chaos Synchronization for Liu-Chen-Liu and Lü Chaotic Systems

Sundarapandian Vaidyanathan[1] and Suresh Rasappan[2]

Vel Tech Dr. RR & Dr. SR Technical University, Avadi-Vel Tech Road, Avadi,
Chennai-600 062, Tamil Nadu, India
Tel.: +91-44-26841622; Fax: +91-44-26840605
sundarvtu@gmail.com

Abstract. This paper investigates the global chaos synchronization of two identical Liu-Chen-Liu chaotic systems (2007) and two different chaotic systems, namely, Liu-Chen-Liu chaotic system (2007) and Lü chaotic system (2002). Nonlinear control is an effective method for making two identical chaotic systems or two different chaotic systems synchronized. Since the Lyapunov exponents are not required for the calculations, this method is an effective and convenient to synchronize two identical and different chaotic systems. Numerical simulations are also given to validate the proposed synchronization approach.

1 Introduction

Chaos synchronization is an important topic in the nonlinear control systems. Synchronization of chaotic systems is an active research problem developed and studied extensively in the last few decades ([1]-[17]). The idea of synchronizing two identical chaotic systems was first introduced by Carroll and Pecora ([1]-[2]). Synchronization has been widely explored in a variety of fields including physical [3], chemical [4], ecological [5] systems, secure communications ([6]-[8]) etc.

In most of the synchronization approaches, the master-slave or drive-response formalism is used. If a particular chaotic system is called the master or drive system and another chaotic system is called the slave or response system, then the idea of synchronization is to use the output of the master system to control the response of the slave system so that the slave system tracks the output of the master system asymptotically. Since the seminal work by Carroll and Pecora [1], a variety of impressive approaches have been proposed for the synchronization of chaotic systems such as PC method ([1]-[2]), sampled-data feedback synchronization method [9], OGY method [10], time-delay feedback approach [11], backstepping design method [12], adaptive design method ([13]-14]), sliding mode control method [15], etc.

This paper is organized as follows. In Section 2, the methodology of chaotic synchronization by nonlinear control method is given. In Section 3, the chaos synchronization of two identical Liu-Chen-Liu chaotic systems is discussed. In Section 4, the chaos synchronization of Liu-Chen-Liu and Lü chaotic systems is discussed. Section 5 gives the conclusions of this paper.

V. V Das, J. Stephen, and N. Thankachan et al. (Eds.): PEIE 2010, CCIS 102, pp. 20–27, 2010.
© Springer-Verlag Berlin Heidelberg 2010

2 Problem Statement and Methodology

Consider the chaotic system described by the dynamics

$$\dot{x} = Ax + f(x) \tag{1}$$

where $x \in R^n$ is the state of the system, A is the $n \times n$ matrix of the system parameters and $f : R^n \to R^n$ is the nonlinear part of the system. The system (1) is considered as the *master* or *drive* system. Also, the chaotic system described by the dynamics

$$\dot{y} = By + g(y) + u \tag{2}$$

is considered the *slave* or *response* system, where $y \in R^n$ is the state vector of the slave system, B is the $n \times n$ matrix of the system parameters, $g : R^n \to R^n$ is the nonlinear part of the slave system and $u \in R^n$ is the nonlinear controller of the slave system. If $A = B$ and $f = g$, then x and y are the states of two identical chaotic systems. If $A \neq B$ and $f \neq g$, then x and y are the states of two different chaotic systems. The global chaos synchronization problem is to design a controller which synchronizes the states of the master system (1) and the slave system (2) for all initial conditions $x(0), y(0) \in R^n$. The synchronization error is defined as

$$e = y - x \tag{3}$$

Then the synchronization error dynamics is obtained as

$$\dot{e} = By - Ax + g(y) - f(x) + u \tag{4}$$

Thus, the global synchronization problem is essentially to find a controller u so as to stabilize the error dynamics (4) for all initial conditions $e(0) \in R^n$, i.e.

$\lim_{t \to \infty} \|e(t)\| = 0$ for all initial conditions $e(0) \in R^n$.

This paper uses Lyapunov function methodology for the synchronization of master system (1) and slave system (2). By the Lyapunov function methodology, a candidate Lyapunov function is taken as

$$V(e) = e^T P e, \tag{5}$$

where P is a $n \times n$ positive definite matrix. Note that $V : R^n \to R^n$ is a positive definite function by construction. It is assumed that the parameters of the master and slave systems are known and that the states of both systems (1) and (2) are measurable. If a controller u can be found such that

$$\dot{V}(e) = -e^T Q e, \tag{6}$$

where Q is a positive definite matrix, then $\dot{V} : R^n \to R^n$ is a negative definite function. Hence, by Lyapunov stability theory [20], the error dynamics (4) is globally exponentially stable and hence the condition (5) will be satisfied for all initial conditions

$e(0) \in R^n$. Then the states of the master system (1) and the slave system (2) are globally exponentially synchronized.

3 Synchronization of Two Identical Liu-Chen Liu Systems

In this section, the nonlinear control method is applied for the synchronization of two identical Liu-Chen-Liu chaotic systems [18]. The Liu-Chen-Liu system (2007) is taken as the master system, which is described by the equations

$$\dot{x}_1 = a(x_2 - x_1)$$
$$\dot{x}_2 = bx_1 + kx_1 x_3 \quad (7)$$
$$\dot{x}_3 = -cx_3 - hx_1 x_2$$

where a, b, c, h and k are positive real constants. The Liu-Chen-Liu system (2007) is also taken as the slave system, which is described by the equations

$$\dot{y}_1 = a(y_2 - y_1) + u_1$$
$$\dot{y}_2 = by_1 + ky_1 y_3 + u_2 \quad (8)$$
$$\dot{y}_3 = -cy_3 - hy_1 y_2 + u_3$$

where $u = [u_1, u_2, u_3]^T$ is the nonlinear controller to be designed so as to synchronize the states of the identical Liu-Chen-Liu systems (8) and (9).

The synchronization error is defined by

$$e_1 = y_1 - x_1, \quad e_2 = y_2 - x_2, \quad e_3 = y_3 - x_3 \quad (9)$$

The error dynamics is obtained as

$$\dot{e}_1 = a(e_2 - e_1) + u_1$$
$$\dot{e}_2 = be_1 + k(y_1 y_3 - x_1 x_3) + u_2 \quad (10)$$
$$\dot{e}_3 = -ce_3 - h(y_1 y_2 - x_1 x_2) + u_3$$

The candidate Lyapunov function is taken as

$$V(e) = \frac{1}{2} e^T e = \frac{1}{2}\left(e_1^2 + e_2^2 + e_3^2\right) \quad (11)$$

A simple calculation gives

$$\dot{V}(e) = ae_1(e_2 - e_1) + e_1 u_1 + be_1 e_2 + ke_2(y_1 y_3 - x_1 x_3)$$
$$+ e_2 u_2 - ce_3^2 - he_3(y_1 y_2 - x_1 x_2) + e_3 u_3 \quad (12)$$

We choose

$$u_1 = -(a+b)e_2$$
$$u_2 = -e_2 + k(x_1 x_3 - y_1 y_3) \tag{13}$$
$$u_3 = h(y_1 y_2 - x_1 x_2)$$

Substitution of (13) into (12) yields

$$\dot{V}(e) = -ae_1^2 - e_2^2 - ce_3^2 \tag{14}$$

which is a negative definite function on R^3 since $a, c > 0$. Hence, by Lyapunov stability theory [20], then the error dynamics (13) is globally exponentially stable. Thus, we have proved the following result.

Theorem 1. The identical Liu-Chen-Liu chaotic systems (7) and (8) are exponentially and globally synchronized for any initial conditions with the nonlinear controller u defined by (13). ∎

Numerical Results

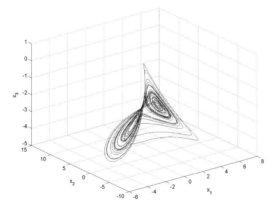

Fig. 1. Chaotic Portrait of the Liu-Chen-Liu System

For the numerical simulations, the fourth-order Runge-Kutta method is used to solve the system using MATLAB. For the Liu-Chen-Liu chaotic system (7), the parameter values are taken as those which result in chaotic behaviour of the system. When $a = 10$, $b = 40$, $c = 2.5$, $h = 1$ and $k = 16$, the Liu-Chen-Liu system (7) has a reversed butterfly-shaped attractor as shown in Figure 1.

The initial values of the master system (7) are taken as $x_1(0) = 1$, $x_2(0) = 9$ and $x_3(0) = 2$, while the initial values of the slave system (8) are taken as $y_1(0) = 9$, $y_2(0) = -3$ and $y_3(0) = -2$. Figure 2 shows that the synchronization between the states of the master system (7) and the slave system (8) occur in 2 seconds.

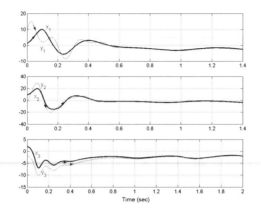

Fig. 2. Synchronization of the Identical Liu-Chen-Liu Systems

4 Synchronization of Liu- Chen-Liu and Lu Chaotic Systems

In this section, the nonlinear control method is applied for the synchronization of two different chaotic systems described by Lü system [19] as the *master* or *drive* system and the Liu-Chen-Liu system [18] as the *slave* or *response* system. The dynamics of the Lü system, taken as the master system, is described by

$$\dot{x}_1 = \alpha(x_2 - x_1)$$
$$\dot{x}_2 = \gamma x_2 - x_1 x_3 \qquad (15)$$
$$\dot{x}_3 = x_1 x_2 - \beta x_3$$

where α, β and γ are positive constants.

The dynamics of the Liu-Chen-Liu system, taken as the slave system, is described by

$$\dot{y}_1 = a(y_2 - y_1) + u_1$$
$$\dot{y}_2 = by_1 + ky_1 y_3 + u_2 \qquad (16)$$
$$\dot{y}_3 = -cy_3 - hy_1 y_2 + u_3$$

where $a,\ b,\ c,\ h,\ k$ are positive constants and $u = \begin{bmatrix} u_1, u_2, u_3 \end{bmatrix}^T$ is the nonlinear controller to be designed so as to synchronize the states of the different chaotic systems (15) and (16). The synchronization error is defined by

$$e_1 = y_1 - x_1, \quad e_2 = y_2 - x_2, \quad e_3 = y_3 - x_3 \qquad (17)$$

The error dynamics is obtained as

$$\dot{e}_1 = a(y_2 - y_1) - \alpha(x_2 - x_1) + u_1$$
$$\dot{e}_2 = by_1 - \gamma x_2 + ky_1 y_3 + x_1 x_3 + u_2 \qquad (18)$$
$$\dot{e}_3 = -cy_3 + \beta x_3 - hy_1 y_2 - x_1 x_2 + u_3$$

The candidate Lyapunov function is taken as

$$V(e) = \frac{1}{2}e^T e = \frac{1}{2}\left(e_1^2 + e_2^2 + e_3^2\right) \qquad (19)$$

A simple calculation gives

$$\dot{V}(e) = ae_1(y_2 - y_1) - \alpha e_1(x_2 - x_1) + e_1 u_1 + be_2 y_1 - \gamma e_2 x_2 + e_2(ky_1 y_3 + x_1 x_3) \qquad (20)$$
$$+ e_2 u_2 - ce_3 y_3 + \beta e_3 x_3 - e_3(hy_1 y_2 + x_1 x_2) + e_3 u_3$$

We choose

$$u_1 = (\alpha - a)(x_2 - x_1) - (a + b)e_2$$
$$u_2 = -e_2 - bx_1 + \gamma x_2 - ky_1 y_3 - x_1 x_3 \qquad (21)$$
$$u_3 = (c - \beta)x_3 + hy_1 y_2 + x_1 x_2$$

Substitution of (21) into (20) yields

$$\dot{V}(e) = -ae_1^2 - e_2^2 - ce_3^2 \qquad (22)$$

which is a negative definite function on R^3 since $a, c > 0$. Hence, by Lyapunov stability theory [20], then the error dynamics (18) is globally exponentially stable.

Thus, we have proved the following result.

Theorem 2. The Lü chaotic system (15) and the Liu-Chen-Liu chaotic system (16) are exponentially and globally synchronized for any initial conditions with the nonlinear controller u defined by (21). ∎

Numerical Results

For the numerical simulations, the fourth-order Runge-Kutta method is used to solve the system using MATLAB. For the Lü chaotic system (15), the parameter values are taken as those which result in chaotic behavior of the system. When $\alpha = 36$, $\beta = 3$ and $\gamma = 20$, the Lü system (15) has chaotic behavior as shown in Figure 3.

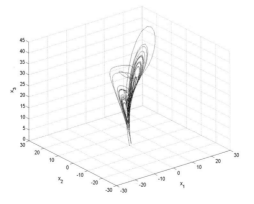

Fig. 3. Chaotic Portrait for Lü System

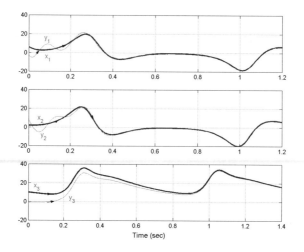

Fig. 4. Synchronization of Liu-Chen-Liu and Lü Chaotic Systems

The initial values of the master system (15) are taken as $x_1(0) = 6$, $x_2(0) = 2$ and $x_3(0) = 10$, while the initial values of the slave system (16) are taken as $y_1(0) = -3$, $y_2(0) = 8$ and $y_3(0) = -1$. Figure 4 shows that the synchronization between the states of the master system (15) and the slave system (16) occur in 1.2 seconds.

5 Conclusions

In this paper, nonlinear control method based on Lyapunov stability theory is proposed to synchronize two identical chaotic systems, namely Liu-Chen-Liu chaotic system (2007) and two different chaotic systems, namely Lü system (2002) and Liu-Chen-Liu chaotic system (2007). Numerical simulations are also given to validate the proposed synchronization approach for the global synchronization of chaotic systems. Since the Lyapunov exponents are not required for the calculation, the proposed nonlinear control method is effective and convenient to synchronize chaotic systems.

References

[1] Carroll, T.L., Pecora, L.M.: Synchronization in chaotic systems. Phys. Rev. Lett. 64, 821–824 (1990)
[2] Carroll, T.L., Pecora, L.M.: Synchronizing chaotic circuits. IEEE Trans. Circ. Sys. 38, 453–456 (1991)
[3] Lakshmanan, M., Murali, K.: Chaos in Nonlinear Oscillators: Controlling and Synchronization. World Scientific, Singapore (1996)
[4] Han, S.K., Kerrer, C., Kuramoto, Y.: Dephasing and bursting in coupled neural oscillators. Phys. Rev. Lett. 75, 3190–3193 (1995)

[5] Blasius, B., Huppert, A., Stone, L.: Complex dynamics and phase synchronization in spatially extended ecological system. Nature 399, 354–359 (1999)

[6] Murali, K., Lakshmanan, M.: Secure communication using a compound signal from generalized synchronizable chaotic systems. Physics Letters A 241, 303–310 (1998)

[7] Cuomo, K.M., Oppenheim, A.V.: Circuit implementation of synchronized chaos with application to communication. Phys. Rev. Lett. 71, 65–68 (1993)

[8] Kocarev, L., Parlitz, U.: General approach for chaotic synchronization with application to communication. Phys. Rev. Lett. 74, 5028–5031 (1995)

[9] Lu, J.A., Xie, J., Lu, J., Chen, S.H.: Control chaos in transition system using sampled-data feedback. Applied Mathematics and Mechanics 24, 1309–1315 (2006)

[10] Ott, E., Grebogi, C., Yorke, J.A.: Controlling chaos. Phys. Rev. Lett. 64, 1196–1199 (1990)

[11] Lu, J., Wu, X., Han, X., Lu, J.: Adaptive feedback synchronization of a unified chaotic system. Phys. Lett. A 329, 327–333 (2004)

[12] Park, J.H., Kwon, O.M.: A novel criterion for delayed feedback control of time-delay chaotic systems. Chaos, Solitons and Fractals 17, 709–716 (2003)

[13] Wu, X., Lu, J.: Parameter identification and backstepping control of uncertain Lu system. Chaos, Solitons and Fractals 18, 721–729 (2003)

[14] Yu, Y.G., Zhang, S.C.: Adaptive backstepping synchronization of uncertain chaotic systems. Chaos, Solitons and Fractals 27, 1369–1375 (2006)

[15] Yau, H.T.: Design of adaptive sliding mode controller for chaos synchronization with uncertainties. Chaos, Solitons and Fractals 22, 341–347 (2004)

[16] Agiza, H.N., Yassen, M.T.: Synchronization of Rössler and Chen dynamical systems using active control. Phys. Lett. A 278, 191–197 (2001)

[17] Liu, L., Chen, S.Y., Liu, C.X.: Experimental confirmation of a new reversed butterfly-shaped attractor. Chin. Phys. 16, 1897–1900 (2007)

[18] Lü, J., Chen, G.: A new chaotic attractor coined. International Journal on Bifurcation and Chaos 12, 659–661 (2002)

New Results on the Reduced Order Model Design for the Linear Discrete-Time Control Systems

V. Sundarapandian[1], M. Kavitha[2], and C.S. Ravichandran[3]

[1] Vel Tech Dr. RR & Dr. SR Technical University, Avadi-Vel Tech Road, Avadi,
Chennai-600 062, Tamil Nadu, India
Tel.: +91-44-26841622; Fax: +91-44-26840605
sundarvtu@gmail.com
[2] Vel Tech Dr. RR & Dr. SR Technical University, Avadi-Vel Tech Road, Avadi,
Chennai-600 062, Tamil Nadu, India
Tel.: +91-44-26841622; Fax: +91-44-26840605
[3] Department of Computer Science and Engineering, SSK College of Engineering,
Coimbatore, Tamil Nadu, India

Abstract. In this paper, we obtain the reduced order model for the linear discrete-time control systems using the dominant state of the control systems. Using the reduced order model, we derive necessary and sufficient conditions for the observer design of linear discrete-time control systems. Our method essentially uses the model reduction of the original linear control systems.

1 Introduction

During the past four decades, a significant attention has been paid to the construction of reduced-order observers and stabilization using reduced-order controllers for linear control systems [1-7]. The standard observer design for linear systems either estimates the full state vector or a linear functional of the state vector as originally proposed by Luenberger [1]. As far as the stabilization of linear control systems is concerned, the state vector may not be available for measurement and so when the linear control system is both controllable and observable, we use the separation principle for linear control systems and use an estimate of the state in lieu of the state vector. This approach works well with small-scale linear systems. However, for large-scale linear systems, the order of the observer is comparable with the order of the observed state dynamics. As a consequence, the observer design problem for large-scale linear control systems involves potential numerical and practical difficulties, and so the state feedback control laws using an estimate of the state in lieu of the state vector may not yield the desired stabilization results.

In this paper, we derive a reduced-order model for any linear discrete-time control system and our approach is based on the approach of using the dominant state of the given linear discrete-time control system, *i.e.* we derive the reduced-order model for a given linear discrete-time control system keeping only the dominant state of the given linear plant. The dominant state of a linear control system corresponds to the *slow modes* of the linear system, while the non-dominant state of the control system corresponds to the *fast modes* of the linear system [4-5, 7-10].

V. V Das, J. Stephen, and N. Thankachan et al. (Eds.): PEIE 2010, CCIS 102, pp. 28–36, 2010.
© Springer-Verlag Berlin Heidelberg 2010

As an application of our recent work [9], we first derive the reduced-order model of the given linear discrete-time control system. Using the reduced-order model obtained, we characterize the existence of a reduced-order exponential observer that tracks the state of the reduced-order model, i.e. the dominant state of the original linear plant. We note that the model reduction and the reduced-order observer design detailed in this paper are discrete-time analogs of the results of Aldeen and Trinh [7] for the observer design of the dominant state of continuous-time linear control systems.

This paper is organized as follows. In Section 2, we derive the reduced-order plant of a given linear discrete-time control system. In Section 3, we derive necessary and sufficient conditions for the exponential observer design for the reduced-order linear control plant. In Section 4, we present an example to illustrate the main results of this paper, viz. deriving the reduced order model for a linear discrete-time plant. In Section 5, we summarize the results obtained in this paper.

2 Reduced Model for the Linear System

Consider a linear discrete-time control system S_1 given by

$$x(k+1) = A\,x(k) + B\,u(k)$$
$$y(k) \;\; = C\,x(k)$$
(1)

where $x \in R^n$ is the *state*, $y \in R^p$ the *output* and $u \in R^m$ the *input* of the linear control system (1).First, we suppose that we have performed an identification of the *dominant* and *non-dominant states* of the given linear control system using the *modal approach* as described in [9].Without loss of generality, we may assume that

$$x = \begin{bmatrix} x_1 \\ x_2 \end{bmatrix}$$

where $x_1 \in R^r$ represents the *dominant* state and $x_2 \in R^{n-r}$ represents the *non-dominant* state. Then the system (1) takes the form

$$\begin{bmatrix} x_1(k+1) \\ x_2(k+1) \end{bmatrix} = \begin{bmatrix} A_{11} & A_{12} \\ A_{21} & A_{22} \end{bmatrix} \begin{bmatrix} x_1(k) \\ x_2(k) \end{bmatrix} + \begin{bmatrix} B_1 \\ B_2 \end{bmatrix} u(k)$$

$$y(k) = \begin{bmatrix} C_1 & C_2 \end{bmatrix} \begin{bmatrix} x_1(k) \\ x_2(k) \end{bmatrix}$$
(2)

From (2), we have

$$x_1(k+1) = A_{11}\,x_1(k) + A_{12}\,x_2(k) + B_1\,u(k)$$
$$x_2(k+1) = A_{21}\,x_1(k) + A_{22}\,x_2(k) + B_2\,u(k)$$
$$y(k) \;\; = C_1\,x_1(k) + C_2\,x_2(k)$$
(3)

For the sake of simplicity, we will assume that the matrix A has distinct eigenvalues. We note that this condition is usually satisfied in most practical situations. Then it follows that A is diagonalizable. Thus, we can find a nonsingular matrix P consisting of the n independent eigenvectors of A so that

$$P^{-1}AP = \Lambda$$

where Λ is a diagonal matrix consisting of the n eigenvalues of A. We introduce new coordinates on the state space given by

$$\xi = P^{-1}x \qquad (4)$$

Then the plant takes the form

$$\xi(k+1) = \Lambda\,\xi(k) + P^{-1}B\,u(k)$$
$$y(k) = CP\,\xi(k)$$

Thus, we have

$$\begin{bmatrix} \xi_1(k+1) \\ \xi_2(k+1) \end{bmatrix} = \begin{bmatrix} \Lambda_1 & 0 \\ 0 & \Lambda_2 \end{bmatrix} \begin{bmatrix} \xi_1(k) \\ \xi_2(k) \end{bmatrix} + P^{-1}B\,u(k)$$

$$y(k) = C\,P \begin{bmatrix} \xi_1(k) \\ \xi_2(k) \end{bmatrix} \qquad (5)$$

where Λ_1 and Λ_2 are $r \times r$ and $(n-r)\times(n-r)$ diagonal matrices respectively.

Define matrices Γ_1, Γ_2, Ψ_1 and Ψ_2 by

$$P^{-1}B = \begin{bmatrix} \Gamma_1 \\ \Gamma_2 \end{bmatrix} \quad \text{and} \quad CP = \begin{bmatrix} \Psi_1 & \Psi_2 \end{bmatrix} \qquad (6)$$

where $\Gamma_1 \in R^{r \times m}$, $\Gamma_2 \in R^{(n-r)\times m}$, $\Psi_1 \in R^{p \times r}$ and $\Psi_2 \in R^{p \times (n-r)}$.

From (5) and (6), we see that the plant (3) has the following simple form in the new coordinates (4):

$$\xi_1(k+1) = \Lambda_1\,\xi_1(k) + \Gamma_1\,u(k)$$
$$\xi_2(k+1) = \Lambda_2\,\xi_2(k) + \Gamma_2\,u(k) \qquad (7)$$
$$y(k) = \Psi_1\,\xi_1(k) + \Psi_2\,\xi_2(k)$$

Next, we make the following assumptions:

(H1) As $k \to \infty$, $\xi_2(k+1) \approx \xi_2(k)$, i.e. ξ_2 takes a constant value in the steady-state.

(H2) The matrix $I - \Lambda_2$ is invertible.

Then it follows from (7) that for large values of k, we have

$$\xi_2(k) \approx \Lambda_2 \, \xi_2(k) + \Gamma_2 \, u(k)$$

i.e. $\xi_2(k) \approx (I - \Lambda_2)^{-1} \Gamma_2 \, u(k)$ (8)

Substituting (8) into (7), we get the reduced-order model in the ξ-coordinates as

$$\xi_1(k+1) = \Lambda_1 \, \xi_1(k) + \Gamma_1 \, u(k)$$
$$y(k) = \Psi_1 \, \xi_1(k) + \Psi_2 (I - \Lambda_2)^{-1} \Gamma_2 \, u(k)$$ (9)

We note that (9) represents the reduced-order model of the plant in the new coordinates. To obtain the reduced-order model of the plant in its original coordinates, we proceed as follows. Set

$$P^{-1} = Q = \begin{bmatrix} Q_{11} & Q_{12} \\ Q_{21} & Q_{22} \end{bmatrix}$$

where $Q_{11} \in R^{r \times r}$, $Q_{12} \in R^{r \times (n-r)}$, $Q_{21} \in R^{(n-r) \times r}$ and $Q_{22} \in R^{(n-r) \times (n-r)}$. By the linear change of coordinates (4), it follows that $\xi = P^{-1} x = Q \, x$. Thus, we have

$$\begin{bmatrix} \xi_1(k) \\ \xi_2(k) \end{bmatrix} = Q \begin{bmatrix} x_1(k) \\ x_2(k) \end{bmatrix} = \begin{bmatrix} Q_{11} & Q_{12} \\ Q_{21} & Q_{22} \end{bmatrix} \begin{bmatrix} x_1(k) \\ x_2(k) \end{bmatrix}.$$

Hence, it follows that

$$\xi_1(k) = Q_{11} \, x_1(k) + Q_{12} \, x_2(k)$$
$$\xi_2(k) = Q_{21} \, x_1(k) + Q_{22} \, x_2(k)$$ (10)

Using(8)and(10), we get

$$\xi_2(k) = Q_{21} \, x_1(k) + Q_{22} \, x_2(k) \approx (I - \Lambda_2)^{-1} \Gamma_2 \, u(k).$$ (11)

Next, we make the following assumption.

(H3) *The matrix Q_{22} is invertible.*

Using **(H3)**, the equation (11) may be simplified as

$$x_2(k) \approx -Q_{22}^{-1} Q_{21} \, x_1(k) + Q_{22}^{-1} (I - \Lambda_2)^{-1} \Gamma_2 \, u(k).$$ (12)

To simplify the notation, we define matrices

$$R = -Q_{22}^{-1} Q_{21} \text{ and } S = Q_{22}^{-1} (I - \Lambda_2)^{-1} \Gamma_2$$ (13)

Using (13), the equation (12) may be simplified as

$$x_2(k) \approx R \, x_1(k) + S \, u(k).$$ (14)

Substituting (14) into (13), we obtain the **reduced-order model** S_2 of the given plant S_1 in its original coordinates as

$$
\begin{aligned}
x_1(k+1) &= A_1^* \, x_1(k) + B_1^* \, u(k) \\
y(k) &= C_1^* \, x_1(k) + D_1^* \, u(k)
\end{aligned}
\tag{15}
$$

where the matrices A_1^*, B_1^*, C_1^* and D_1^* are defined by

$$
\begin{aligned}
A_1^* &= A_{11} + A_{12}R \\
B_1^* &= B_1 + A_{12}S \\
C_1^* &= C_1 + C_2 R \\
D_1^* &= C_2 S
\end{aligned}
\tag{16}
$$

3 Reduced Order Observer Design

In this section, we state and prove an important result that prescribes a simple, practical procedure for estimating the dominant-state of the given linear control system that satisfies the assumptions **(H1)--(H3)**.

Theorem 1. *Let S_1 be the linear system described by*

$$
\begin{aligned}
x(k+1) &= A\,x(k) + B\,u(k) \\
y(k) &= C\,x(k)
\end{aligned}
\tag{17}
$$

Under the assumptions **(H1)-(H3)**, the reduced-order model S_2 of the plant S_1 can be obtained [see Section 2] as

$$
\begin{aligned}
x_1(k+1) &= A_1^* \, x_1(k) + B_1^* \, u(k) \\
y(k) &= C_1^* \, x_1(k) + D_1^* \, u(k)
\end{aligned}
\tag{18}
$$

where A_1^*, B_1^*, C_1^* and D_1^* are defined as in (16). To estimate the dominant state of the system S_1, consider the candidate observer S_3 defined by

$$
z_1(k+1) = A_1^* z_1(k) + B_1^* u(k) + K_1^*[y(k) - C_1^* z_1(k) - D_1^* u(k)]
\tag{19}
$$

Define the estimation error as $e \overset{\Delta}{=} z_1 - x_1$. Then $e(k) \to 0$ as $k \to \infty$ if and only if the matrix K_1^* is such that the matrix $A_1^* - K_1^* C_1^*$ is convergent (note that a square matrix E .is defined to be convergent if and only if all the eigenvalues of E

lie inside the open unit disc of the complex plane). If (C_1^*, A_1^*) is observable, then we can construct an observer of the form (19) having any desired speed of convergence.

Proof. From (3), we have

$$x_1(k+1) = A_{11}\, x_1(k) + A_{12}\, x_2(k) + B_1\, u(k). \tag{20}$$

Adding and subtracting $(A_{12} - K_1^* C_2)R\, x_1(k)$ in the R.H.S. of (20), we get

$$x_1(k+1) = (A_{11} + A_{12}R - K_1^*\, C_2\, R)\, x_1(k) - (A_{12} - K_1^* C_2)\, R\, x_1(k) \\ + A_{12}\, x_2(k) + B_1\, u(k) \tag{21}$$

Subtracting (21) from (20), and simplifying using the definitions (16), we have

$$e(k+1) = (A_1^* - K_1^* C_1^*)e(k) - (A_{12} - K_1^* C_2)[x_2(k) - R\, x_1(k) - S\, u(k)]. \tag{21}$$

The assumptions (H1)-(H3) yield $x_2(k) \approx R\, x_1(k) + S\, u(k)$.

Therefore, $e(k+1) \approx (A_1^* - K_1^* C_1^*)\, e(k)$. Hence, it follows that

$$e(k) \approx \left(A_1^* - K_1^* C_1^*\right)^k e(0). \tag{22}$$

From (23), it is immediate that $e(k) \to 0$ as $k \to \infty$ for all values of $e(0)$ if and only if all the eigenvalues of the matrix $A_1^* - K_1^* C_1^*$ lie inside the open unit disc of the complex plane. This completes the proof. ∎

4 Numerical Example

Consider the fourth order discrete-time control system S_1 described by

$$x(k+1) = A\, x(k) + B\, u(k) \\ y(k) = C\, x(k) \tag{23}$$

where

$$A = \begin{bmatrix} 0.8940 & -0.4237 & -0.0083 & 0.0001 \\ 0.4237 & 0.8735 & -0.0296 & 0.0003 \\ -0.0083 & 0.0296 & 0.2328 & 0.0433 \\ -0.0001 & 0.0003 & -0.0433 & 0.1485 \end{bmatrix}$$

$$B = [-0.4214 \quad 0.4474 \quad -0.2296 \quad -0.0025]^T,$$
$$C = [-0.4214 \quad -0.4474 \quad -0.2296 \quad 0.0025].$$

eigenvalues of A are: $\lambda_{1,2} = 0.8835 \pm 0.4241i$, $\lambda_{3,4} = 0.1909 \pm 0.0089i$.

The dominance measure of the eigenvalues is calculated as in [9] and obtained as

$$\Omega = \begin{bmatrix} 15.5459 & 15.5459 & 0.0214 & 0.0214 \\ 15.5578 & 15.5578 & 0.0202 & 0.0202 \\ 0.6105 & 0.6105 & 0.7652 & 0.7652 \\ 0.0263 & 0.0263 & 0.7652 & 0.7652 \end{bmatrix}$$

To determine the dominance of the kth eigenvalue in all the n states, we use the measure (see [9]), $\Theta_k = \sum_{i=1}^{n} \Omega_{ik}$. Thus, we obtain

$$\Theta = \begin{bmatrix} 31.7405 & 31.7405 & 1.5720 & 1.5720 \end{bmatrix}$$

To determine the relative dominance of the kth eigen value in the ith state, we use the measure (see [9]), $\phi_{ik} = \left| \dfrac{\Omega_{ik}}{\Theta_k} \right| \times 100$. Thus, we obtain

$$\Phi = \begin{bmatrix} 48.9781 & 48.9781 & 1.3613 & 1.3613 \\ 49.0156 & 49.0156 & 1.2850 & 1.2850 \\ 1.9234 & 1.9234 & 48.6768 & 48.6768 \\ 0.0829 & 0.0829 & 48.6768 & 48.6768 \end{bmatrix}$$

Thus, it is easy to see that the first two states x_1, x_2 are the dominant states and the last two states x_3, x_4 are the non-dominant states. To find the reduced order model of the plant (24), we first represent the plant (33) in the phase variable form as

$$A = \begin{bmatrix} 0 & 1 & 0 & 0 \\ 0 & 0 & 1 & 0 \\ 0 & 0 & 0 & 1 \\ -0.0351 & 0.4313 & -1.6716 & 2.1488 \end{bmatrix},$$

$$B = \begin{bmatrix} 0 & 0 & 0 & 1 \end{bmatrix}^T, C = \begin{bmatrix} -0.0021 & 0.0035 & 0.0835 & 0.0302 \end{bmatrix}.$$

The reduced order model of this plant using the construction detailed in Section II is obtained as

$$X_1(k+1) = A_1^* X_1(k) + B_1^* u(k)$$
$$y(k) = C_1^* X_1(k) + D_1^* u(k)$$

where

$$A_1^* = \begin{bmatrix} 0 & 1.0000 \\ -0.9604 & 1.7670 \end{bmatrix}, \; B_1^* = \begin{bmatrix} 0 \\ 1.5275 \end{bmatrix}$$

$$C_1^* = \begin{bmatrix} -0.1335 & 0.2163 \end{bmatrix} \text{ and } D_1^* = [0.2551].$$

The step responses of the original plant and the reduced order plant are plotted in Figure 1, which validates the reduced-order model obtained for the given plant

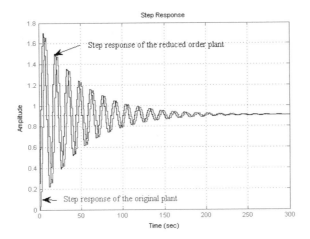

Fig. 1. Step Responses of the Original and Reduced Plants

It is also easy to check that the observability matrix is

$$O(C_1^*, A_1^*) = \begin{bmatrix} -0.1335 & 0.2163 \\ -0.2077 & 0.2487 \end{bmatrix}$$

which also has rank 2. Thus, the reduced order plant is observable.

Hence, we can build a reduced order observer for the given plant using the methods detailed in Sections 3.

5 Conclusions

In this paper, we obtained the reduced-order model for discrete-time linear control systems using the dominant state of the linear systems. Our calculations were carried out by performing an identification of the dominant and non-dominant states of the given linear system using the modal approach as described in (Sundarapandian, 2005). We illustrated our results with an example and plotted the step responses of the original and reduced order state models.

References

[1] Luenberger, D.G.: Observers for multivariable systems. IEEE Trans. Automat. Control 11, 190–197 (1966)
[2] Cumming, S.D.: Design of observers of reduced dynamics. Electronics Letters 5, 213–214 (1969)
[3] Fortman, T.E., Williamson, D.: Design of low-order observers for linear feedback control laws. IEEE Trans. Automat. Control 17, 301–308 (1972)
[4] Lastman, G.J., Sinha, N.K., Rozsa, P.: On the selection of states to be retained in a re-duced-order model. IEE Proceedings – Control Theory 131, 15–24 (1984)
[5] Litz, L., Roth, H.: State decomposition for singular perturbation order reduction – a modal approach. International J. Control 34, 937–954 (1981)
[6] Murdoch, P.: Observer design of a linear functional of the state vector. IEEE Trans. Automat. Control 18, 308–310 (1973)
[7] Aldeen, M., Trinh, H.: Observing a subset of the states of linear systems. IEE Proceedings – Control Theory 141, 137–144 (1994)
[8] Aldeen, M.: Interaction modelling approach to distributed control with application to power systems. International J. Control 53, 1035–1044 (1991)
[9] Sundarapandian, V.: Distributed control schemes for large-scale interconnected discrete-time linear systems. Mathematical and Computer Modelling 41, 313–319 (2005)

Transient Stability Enhancement of a Multimachine Power System with Admittance Model Static Reactive Power Compensator

Jose P. Therattil and P.C. Panda

Electrical Engineering Department, National Institute of Technology, Rourkela, India
josetherattil@yahoo.co.in

Abstract. In the proposed work, the effectiveness of the power system stabilizer and static var compensator is analyzed. Synchronous machines are represented by detailed flux linkage model. The equations of the interconnecting network are expressed with regards to a synchronously rotating common reference frame. Equations of synchronous machine, voltage regulator and speed governor are solved in Park's reference frame fixed to the field of each individual machine. It is shown that static reactive-power controller can improve synchronizing and damping torque considerably. The effectiveness of the controllers is demonstrated on a two machine system with a simplified tie line by creating an abnormal operating condition, a 3-phase short circuit. Simulation results are presented at the end of the paper.

Keywords: Excitation control, Power System Stabilizer, Transient Stability.

1 Introduction

Power system must be carefully controlled in order to maintain an acceptable power supply quality. Transient stability of synchronous generators can be improved by excitation systems. This however deteriorates synchronous generator damping. The basic function of a power system stabilizer (PSS) is to add damping to the generator rotor oscillations by controlling its excitation using auxiliary stabilizing signal [1]. While excitation controllers are normally effective in damping power oscillations, they suffer a drawback of being liable to cause a great variation in the voltage profile.

Thyristor-controlled reactors and capacitors, termed as static Var compensators (SVC) are well known to improve power system properties such as stability limits, voltage regulation, Var compensation, etc. Voltage controlled SVC, as such, does not provide any damping. However an additional signal through SVC voltage control loop has been observed to provide extra damping. This paper proposes an admittance model SVC. In this the voltage feedback control is useful for increasing the synchronizing power and the use of an auxiliary stabilizing signal is useful for increasing the damping force.

Equations describing the behavior of the entire power system are developed on the basis of a hybrid reference frame. Machines are connected to the network at the specified nodes, at which voltages and currents in the two reference frames are related to

V. V Das, J. Stephen, and N. Thankachan et al. (Eds.): PEIE 2010, CCIS 102, pp. 37–41, 2010.
© Springer-Verlag Berlin Heidelberg 2010

one another by axis transformation [2]. During any disturbance, speed of machines change and hence their individual reference frames oscillate with respect to the synchronously rotating common reference frame.

1.1 Description of Synchronous Machine

Complete description of the dynamic behavior of the synchronous machine requires consideration of its electrical and mechanical characteristics as well as those of associated control systems. In the proposed work saturation effects are neglected. In most stability analyses, the terms $P_{\psi d}$ and $P_{\psi q}$ are equated to zero. In the proposed simulation they are included [3], hence network equations can be solved separately which involves only matrix multiplication. The flux linkage equations for numerical integration are:

$$p\psi_{fd} = \omega_0 \left[\frac{r_{fd}}{x_{ad}} E_{fd} + \frac{r_{fd}}{x_{fl}} (\psi_{ad} - \psi_{fd}) \right] . \qquad \qquad \text{(1)}$$

$$p\psi_d = \omega_0 \left[e_d + \psi_q \frac{\omega}{\omega_0} + \frac{r}{x_{al}} (\psi_{ad} - \psi_d) \right] . \qquad \qquad \text{(2)}$$

$$p\psi_{kd} = \omega_0 \frac{r_{kd}}{x_{kdl}} (\psi_{ad} - \psi_{kd}) . \qquad \qquad \text{(3)}$$

$$p\psi_q = \omega_0 \left[e_q - \psi_d \frac{\omega}{\omega_0} + \frac{r}{x_{al}} (\psi_{aq} - \psi_q) \right] . \qquad \qquad \text{(4)}$$

$$p\psi_{kq} = \omega_0 \frac{r_{kq}}{x_{kql}} (\psi_{aq} - \psi_{kq}) . \qquad \qquad \text{(5)}$$

Similarly, mechanical and control system equations are

$$p(p\alpha) = \frac{1}{M} [T_i - T_g - K_d(p\alpha) - \Delta T] . \qquad \qquad \text{(6)}$$

$$p(\alpha) = (p\alpha) . \qquad \qquad \text{(7)}$$

$$p(E_{fd}) = \frac{1}{\tau_e} [\mu(V_r - e_t - v_s) - E_{fd}] . \qquad \qquad \text{(8)}$$

$$P(\Delta T) = \frac{1}{\tau_h} \left\{ K_h \left(\frac{\omega - \omega_0}{\omega_0} \right) - \Delta T \right\} . \qquad \qquad \text{(9)}$$

$$pv_2 = K_{STAB} p\Delta\omega_r - \frac{1}{T_{W1}} v_2 . \qquad \qquad \text{(10)}$$

$$pv_s = \frac{T_1}{T_2} pv_2 + \frac{1}{T_2} v_2 - \frac{1}{T_2} v_s . \qquad \qquad \text{(11)}$$

The terminal currents required for connection with the network are

$$i_d = \frac{1}{x_{al}} (\psi_{ad} - \psi_d) . \qquad \qquad \text{(12)}$$

$$i_q = \frac{1}{x_{al}} (\psi_{aq} - \psi_q) . \qquad \qquad \text{(13)}$$

The behavior of the entire power system is expressed by one such set of equations for each machine together with the terminal constraints imposed by the interconnecting network [4]. In the process of computation, voltages e_d and e_q which result from network constraints and appear as nonintegrable variables in machine equations, are considered as the input quantities for the solution of the machine differential equations, where as currents I_d and I_q are looked upon as their output quantities.

1.2 Static Reactive Power Compensator

A static var compensator is a static var generator whose output is varied so as to maintain or control specific parameters of the electric power systems. Most of the presently used thyristor-controlled static var generators in effect provide a variable shunt impedance by synchronously switching shunt capacitors and or reactors "in" and "out" of the network. Using appropriate switch control, the var output can be controlled continuously from maximum capacitive to maximum inductive output at a given network voltage. Static reactive-power controllers [5] are finding wider use in transmission-system applications. In higher-power industrial applications, static reactive power systems are a well established means of reactive power control. Many different static reactive-power system configurations are possible. The choice of a configuration depends on a number of factors: reactive-power requirements, loss characteristics, harmonic generation and cost. The input signals to the above models are the bus bar voltage change and the auxiliary speed or other measurable signal at the voltage-controlled bus bar of the system, and the output of the control system is the firing-angle change required for control of the admittance presented to the system. However, in all these models the gains and time constants and various regulator parameters are to be designed by a trial and error method and will vary depending on the system configuration.

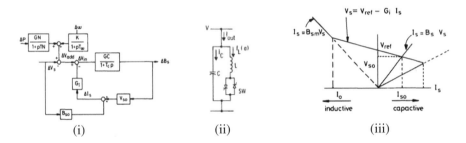

Fig. 1. Static Reactive- Power Compensator (i) Block diagram, (ii) Single-phase schematic diagram, (iii) V/I characteristics

From the figure the steady-state operating point of the SVC is given by the point of intersection of two straight lines such that

$$I_s = B_s v_s \ . \qquad\qquad\qquad \text{............... (14)}$$

$$v_s = v_{ref} - G_I I_s \ . \qquad\qquad\qquad \text{................. (15)}$$

Where v_s is the terminal voltage, I_s is the reactive output current, B_s is the equivalent admittance and v_{ref} is the reference voltage for the SVC
Linearised form of equation (14) is

$$\Delta I_s = B_{so}\Delta v_s + v_{so}\Delta B_s \ . \qquad\qquad\qquad \text{............. (16)}$$

Where Δ denotes a small variation. Furthermore the input signal Δv_i to the main control circuit of the SVC is

$$\Delta v_i = -\Delta v_s - G_I\Delta I_s + \Delta v_{add} \ . \qquad\qquad\qquad \text{................ (17)}$$

Where Δv_{add} a stabilizing signal is derived from generator speed and active power deviations of the SVC bus bar and is given by

$$\Delta v_{add} = \left[\frac{-G_N}{1+sT_n}\right]\Delta p + \left[\frac{G_\omega}{1+sT_\omega}\right]\Delta\omega \ . \qquad\qquad \dots\dots\dots\dots \ (18)$$

From equations (16) and (17) we obtain

$$p\Delta B_s = -\frac{1}{T_c}(1 + G_I G_C v_{so})\Delta B_s - \frac{G_c}{T_c}(1 + G_I B_{so})\Delta v_s + \frac{G_c}{T_c}\Delta v_{add} \ . \qquad \dots\dots\dots\dots \ (19)$$

Where G_I, G_C and G_N are the various gains, and T_c, T_ω and T_n are the time constants

2 Case Study

To illustrate the effectiveness of the PSS and SVC, a 2-machine power system is considered. Generator-1, the machine being investigated, is considered in detailed model [6]. Generator-2, machine away from point of interest, is represented by a fixed voltage behind its transient reactance. Generator-1 is equipped with a conventional voltage regulator and speed governor. The two machine system described in Figure-2(a) was specified quite arbitrarily; but it is intended to be representative of typical real systems which normally have a wide range of tie-line strengths. The operating point was also selected arbitrarily to give an exaggerated range of terminal voltages and power factors. In this case, the SVC is situated at the terminal of machine-1. The network admittance matrix Y may be written in partitioned form as

$$\begin{bmatrix} I_1 \\ I_2 \end{bmatrix} = \begin{bmatrix} Y_1 & Y_{12} \\ Y_{21} & Y_2 \end{bmatrix} \begin{bmatrix} E_1 \\ E_2 \end{bmatrix} \qquad\qquad \dots\dots \ (20)$$

In the analysis proposed, complete solution of the network is required once for each step of integration. Currents at the nodes associated with machine-1 is known after the solution of machine differential equations; voltage E_2, being fixed in magnitude, is also known. Therefore, the purpose of the network solution is to find voltages E_1 and currents I_2 for use in the next step of integration. For this purpose the equation (20) is rearranged into

$$\begin{bmatrix} E_1 \\ I_2 \end{bmatrix} = \begin{bmatrix} Z_1 & -Z_1 Y_{12} \\ Y_{21} Z_1 & Y_2 - Y_{21} Z_1 Y_{12} \end{bmatrix} \begin{bmatrix} I_1 \\ E_2 \end{bmatrix} \qquad\qquad (21)$$

The transient performance of the power system with PSS and Admittance Model SVC is studied for a Three-Phase fault on the transmission line near machine -2, as shown by point F. The loading condition is P1=0.5, Q1=0.3. The fault logic is such that the fault is happening after 0.5second of the beginning of simulation and persists for 0.15 second. Fault is cleared by disconnecting line-2 from the network by opening the circuit breakers at both ends. Hence the total reactance of the transmission line becomes double throughout the balance simulation. Simulation results are shown in figure 2.

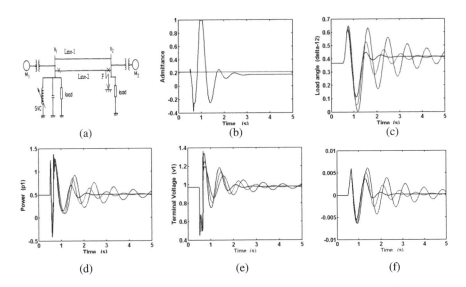

Fig. 2. Sample power system and Dynamic performance, Red-with PSS, Black- SVC

From the figure it is evident that the oscillations in the load angle δ_{12}, active power P_1, terminal voltage V_1, and change in speed $\Delta\omega_1$(Fig-2f) of machine 1 are reduced more considerably with SVC. Peak value of the first power swing is suppressed considerably by the use of SVC .The high gain, quick-response SVC increases the synchronizing power and improves stability better than PSS. SVC provides an external control and hence permits a greater freedom in design. Auxiliary stabilizing signals can be easily incorporated in a static compensator control circuit. Application of a static compensator at transmission line improves power transfer capabilities.

References

1. Anderson, P.M., Fouad, A.A.: Power system Control and Stability. Iowa State University Press, AMES, U.S.A (1977)
2. Kundur, P.: Power System Stability and Control. McGraw-Hill, New York (1944)
3. Prabhashankar, K., Janischewsyj, W.: Digital Simulation of Multimachine Power System for Stability Studies. Trans. IEEE, PAS 87(1) (January 1968)
4. Shackshaft, G.: General Purpose Turbo Alternator Model. Proc. IEEE (London) 110, 703–713 (1963)
5. Dash, P.K., Panda, P.C., Sharaf, A.M.: Adaptive Controller for Static Reactive-Power compensators in Power System. Proc. IEE 134, Pt.C (3) (May 1987)
6. Park, R.H.: Two Reaction Theory of Synchronous Machines-II. Trans. AIEE 52, 352–355 (1933)

Design of Cranial Electrotherapy Stimulator and Analyzing It with EEG

Gopalakrishnan Narayanamurthy and Mahesh Veezhinathan

Department of Biomedical Engineering, SSN College of Engineering, Chennai
maheshv@ssn.edu.in

Abstract. To design a portable low cost Cranial Electrotherapy Stimulator (CES) and to study the corresponding brain activity electrically. The designed stimulator was used as an external trigger and the impact was analyzed using 20 lead EEG electrode system with standard recording protocol. Subjects were tested under this and their corresponding normal and varying EEG with CES were noted. Result showed appreciable variation in the EEG signal when CES evoking potential was connected. The test was carried out for normal subjects in a selected age group. This test should also be done with huge population of diverse age groups and also for abnormal subjects. The results also confirm that this CES could be used in treatment for therapeutic reasons like anxiety, depression, insomnia, and chemical dependency.

Keywords: EEG, CES, trigger and evoking potential.

1 Introduction

Electroencephalography is the study of recording the electrical signals generated by the brain. It is a graphic display of the difference in voltages developed between two sites of functional brain which is recorded over time. The placement of electrodes for recording is done in accordance with the international 10-20 electrode system which uses anatomical landmarks on the skull [1]. The landmarks referred by the system are (a) nasion at the forehead (b) inion at the back and (c) the tragus on both the ears [2]. By utilizing this system the electrodes are placed at specific points in the four lobes namely frontal, parietal, occipital and central lobes. EEG thus provides a broad survey of the electro cerebral activity and indications of cerebral dysfunctions from both the hemispheres. Cranial Electrotherapy Stimulation (CES) is a safe, non-drug approach to treat depression, anxiety, and insomnia. Like many drugs, its exact mechanisms are not known [3]. Its tiny "micro currents" are thought to stimulate the areas of the brain responsible for neurotransmitter and hormone production. Cranial electrotherapy stimulation (CES) is a noninvasive procedure that has been used for decades in the United States to treat anxiety, depression, and insomnia in the general population [4-5]. Whether CES is an effective treatment for patients with a DSM-IV diagnosis of generalized anxiety disorder (GAD) has not previously been explored [6]. In this work CES was designed and was subjected to a particular age group. The corresponding variations in EEG were also reported.

V. V Das, J. Stephen, and N. Thankachan et al. (Eds.): PEIE 2010, CCIS 102, pp. 42–45, 2010.

2 Methodology

The block diagram of designed CES system is as shown in Fig. 1. The designed unit generates adjustable pulsating current in the order of microamperes. The current flows through the clips connected to earlobes. The output obtained from the device was found to be a positive pulse with time period in milliseconds and was followed by a negative one of the same duration. This sequence of positive and negative pulse repeats with a time gap of few seconds. The main frequency of the sequence was of certain hertz. This kind of minute specialized electrical impulses contributes to achieve a varying EEG [7].

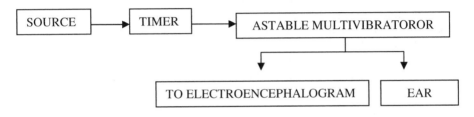

Fig. 1. Block diagram of stimulation and EEG recording

The working system consists of two separate modules as shown in Fig.2 and Fig.3. Evoke potential circuit (fig.2) consists of a Timer which forms a narrow pulse, 2.5Hz oscillator feeding the astable multivibrator. A variation in the circuit can be done by replacing the circuit with high speed operational amplifiers to produce pulses of accurate frequencies. This vibrator generates the various timings for the output pulses. Output was taken at multivibrator with the help of ear clips to easily obtain negative going pulses also.

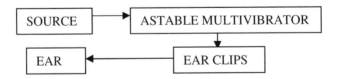

Fig. 2. Block diagram of evoke potential circuit

Current output was limited as required using a limiting resistor and was regulated by means of another resistor. The LED flashes at the end of every cycle signaling proper operation and can also be used for time period setting purposes. It can be omitted together with another resistor, greatly increasing the battery life.

Basic EEG measurement system is as shown in Fig.3 [8].

Fig. 3. Block diagram of EEG measurement

This system consists of electrode placement in standard 10-20 format to obtain the EEG signal [9]. The signal was transferred to the PC using a data cable for further analysis. The EEG output obtained was analyzed for the variations with that of EEG taken without evoke potential [10].

3 Result and Discussion

A simple low cost portable Cranial Electrotherapy Stimulator (CES) set for varying the brain activity electrically was designed and tested for change in EEG signal simultaneously. The test was carried out in a selected population under standard recording protocol [11]. Ear-clips was made with little plastic clips with large surface area to reduce the impedance [12] .The end of the wire was cemented in a position to make good contact with minimum impedance at the earlobes. The subject under test was provided with evoke potential at the earlobes and the EEG recording was carried out in normal and CES conditions (Signal not presented). An EMG notch filter was used to remove the unwanted muscle potential. The changes in EEG were noted.

4 Conclusion

The designed circuit was tested with certain age group and analyzed for change in the EEG. To achieve higher accuracy the study need to be carried over huge population of different age groups. The test can also be carried out for abnormal subjects and could be diagnosed for their recovery. To ensure better current transfer, devices usually have felt pads moistened with a conducting solution interposed between clips and skin [13]. The results were encouraging and with more subjects analyzed with this CES system, this could well be utilized by a physician as a diagnostic tool.

References

1. Tyner, F.S., Knott, J.R., Knott, J.R., Brem Mayer, W.: Fundamentals of EEG Technology: Basic concepts and methods. Medical 1, 144–148 (1983)
2. Tatum, W.O., Husain, A.M., Benbadis, S.R.: Handbook of EEG Interpretation: Normal EEG. Demos medical. Craig percy, Richard Johnson 1, 1–50 (2008)
3. Bystritsky, A., Kerwin, L., Feusner, J.: A pilot study of cranial electrotherapy stimulation for generalized anxiety disorder. J. Clinical Psychiatry 69, 412–417 (2008)
4. Childs, A., Lynn Crismon, M.: The Use of Cranial Electrotherapy Stimulation in Post-Traumatic Amnesia: A Report of Two Cases. Brain Injury 2, 243–247 (1988)
5. Schmitt, R., Capo, T., Boyd, E.: Cranial Electrotherapy Stimulation as a Treatment for Anxiety in Chemically Dependent Persons. Alcoholism: Clinical and Experimental Research 10, 158–160 (1986)
6. Wilson, W.P.: Applications of electroencephalography in psychiatry: a symposium. Medical 8, 52–55 (1965)
7. Niedermeyer, E., Lopes da Silva, F.H.: Electroencephalography: basic principles, clinical applications, and related fields. Medical 5, 278–282 (2005)
8. Lynn, P.A.: An Introduction to the Analysis and Processing of Signals. Halsted Press (1973)

9. Einthoven: Die galvanometrische Registrirung des menschlichen Elektrokardiogramms, zugleich eine Beurtheilung der Anwendung des Capillar-Elecktrometers in der Physiologie. Pflugers Arch. Ges. Physiol. 99, 472–475 (1903)
10. Brown, R.G.: Introduction to Random Signal Analysis and Kalman Filtering. JohnWiley and Sons, NewYork (1983)
11. Methods of analysis of brain electrical and magnetic Signals. In: Givens, A., Remond, A. (eds.) EEG Handbook, vol. 1. Elsevier, Amsterdam (1987)
12. Bronzino, J.: Quantitative analysis of the EEG: general concepts and animal studies. IEEE Trans. Biomed. Eng. 31(12), 850 (1984)
13. Sullivan, T., Deiss, S., Jung, T.P., Cauwenberghs, G.: A Low-Noise, Low-Power EEG Acquisition Node for Scalable Brain-Machine Interfaces. In: Proceedings of the SPIE Conference on Bioengineered and Bioinspired Systems III (2007)

Analysis on Static Voltage Stability Using SVC, STATCOM, TCSC & UPFC

S.M. Padmaja[1] and G. Tulasiram Das[2]

[1] Assoc. Professor, Department of Electrical & Electronics Engg,
Shri Vishnu Engineering College for Women, Bhimavaram, W.G.Dt, AP, India
padmaja_vvr@yahoo.com
[2] Professor, Department of Electrical Engineering,
Jawaharlal Nehru Technological University, Hyderabad, AP, India -500085
das_tulasiram@yahoo.co.in

Abstract. Modern electric power utilities are facing many challenges due to ever increasing complexity in their operation and structure. One problem that received wide attention is voltage instability. One of the major causes of voltage instability in the power system is with its reactive power limit. Voltage instability is the cause of the system voltage collapse, in which the power system voltage decays to a level, from which point, it is unable to recover. Voltage collapse may lead to partial or full power interruption in the system. Providing adequate reactive power support at the appropriate location solves voltage instability problems.

Improving the systems reactive power handling capacity with Flexible AC Transmission System (FACTS) devices is one remedy for prevention of the voltage instability and voltage collapse. In this paper the effect of four FACTS controllers SVC, STATCOM, TCSC and UPFC on voltage stability are studied. The IEEE-14 bus system is simulated with continuation power flow feature of PSAT and accurate model of these controllers for Voltage stability of a test system is investigated.

Keywords: SVC, STATCOM, TCSC, UPFC, Static Voltage Stability, Continuation Power Flow, Voltage Collapse, Maximum Loading Point.

1 Introduction

Voltage collapse phenomena in power systems are caused due to voltage instability when it is loaded beyond Maximum Loading Point (MLP) [1]. Several reports on PV curves are made with saddle node bifurcations and voltage collapse problems [2].

Based on bifurcation theory, the computation of the collapse point is done through direct or continuation methods [3]. These techniques involve the identification of the system equilibrium points or voltage collapse points where the related power flow Jacobian becomes singular [4], [5].

The reactive compensation level and thus voltage stability of the system is improved by FACTS controllers like static var compensator (SVC), Static Synchronous Compensator (STATCOM), Thyristor Controlled Series Capacitor (TCSC), Static

V. V Das, J. Stephen, and N. Thankachan et al. (Eds.): PEIE 2010, CCIS 102, pp. 46–52, 2010.
© Springer-Verlag Berlin Heidelberg 2010

Synchronous Series Compensator (SSSC) & Unified Power Flow Controller (UPFC)[6].

Canizares and Faur studied the effects of SVC and TCSC on voltage collapse [7]. In [8], voltage stability improvements in the system with shunt compensation devices like shunt capacitors, SVC and STATCOM is compared for the IEEE14-bus test system. Study of STATCOM and UPFC Controllers for Voltage Stability evaluated by Saddle-Node Bifurcation Analysis is carried out in [9].

Based on the above observations, an effort made in this paper is to compare the merits and demerits of some FACTS devices, namely, SVC, STATCOM, TCSC and UPFC, in terms of MLP in static voltage stability study.

In Section II a brief description of the stability models of SVC, STATCOM, TCSC and UPFC is presented. Section III examines the effects of these controllers on voltage stability using an IEEE 14-bus test system. Section IV summarizes the main points discussed in this paper.

2 Model of FACTS Controllers

Each of the FACTS devices has its own characteristics giving different levels of benefits in terms of voltage stability margin. The general model proposed for representation of SVC, STATCOM, TCSC and UPFC in voltage collapse studies: [6].

$$\dot{X}_c = f_c(X_c, V, \theta, u); \; P = g_p(X_c, V, \theta); \quad Q = g_p(X_c, V, \theta) \tag{1}$$

Where X_c represents control system variables, and the algebraic variables V and θ denote the voltage magnitudes and phases at which the FACTS devices are connected.

A. **SVC:** Fixed capacitor with a thyristor controlled reactor (FC-TCR) is considered in this paper for the analysis of SVC, which is shown in Fig.1

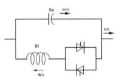   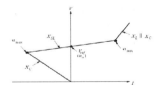

Fig. 1. Equivalent FC-TCR circuit of SVC   **Fig. 2.** Steady state V–I characteristic of a SVC

The TCR consists of a fixed reactor and a bi-directional thyristor valve that are fired symmetrically in an angle (α) control range of 90° to 180°, wrt. the SVC voltage. Performing a Fourier series analysis on the inductor current wave form, the TCR at fundamental frequency can be considered to be equal to a variable inductance X_v given by [7]:

$$X_v = X_L \frac{\pi}{2(\pi - \alpha) + \sin 2\alpha} \tag{2}$$

Hence, the total equivalent impedance of the controller can be represented as:

$$X_e = X_c \frac{\frac{\pi}{r_x}}{\sin 2\alpha - 2\alpha + \pi(2 - 1/r_x)} \tag{3}$$

Where, $r_x = \frac{X_c}{X_L}$, The typical steady-state characteristics SVC is depicted in Fig.2.

A typical value for the controlled voltage range is $\pm 5\%$ about V_{ref} [8].

B. STATCOM: Figs. 3 and 4 shows the basic structure and typical steady state V–I characteristic of STATCOM, respectively. STATCOM is a shunt-connected device, which controls the voltage at the connected bus to the reference value by adjusting voltage and angle of internal voltage source. STATCOM exhibits constant current characteristics when the voltage is low/high about its limit. This type of characteristics allows STATCOM to deliver constant reactive power at the limits.

The power injection at the AC bus has the form:

$P = V^2 G - K V_{dc} V G \cos(\theta - \alpha) - K V_{dc} V B \sin(\theta - \alpha)$; Where $K = \sqrt{3}/8m$

$Q = -V^2 B + K V_{dc} V B \cos(\theta - \alpha) - K V_{dc} V G \sin(\theta - \alpha)$ \hfill (4)

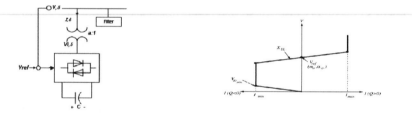

Fig. 3. Basic Structure of STATCOM   **Fig. 4.** V–I characteristic of a STATCOM

C. TCSC: TCSC is the type of series compensator with a capacitive bank and the thyristor controlled inductive branch connected in parallel as shown in Fig. 5. The principle of TCSC is to compensate the transmission line in order to adjust the line impedance, increase loadability, and prevent the voltage collapse [10].

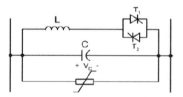

Fig. 5. The basic structure of TCSC

D. UPFC: The basic component of the UPFC are two voltage source inverters (VSI's) sharing a common dc storage capacitor, and connected to the system through coupling transformers (Fig 6). One VSI is connected in shunt to the transmission system via a shunt transformer, while the other one is connected in series through a series transformer. The shunt and series controllers are controlled in a coordinated manner for the exchange of real power via the power link.

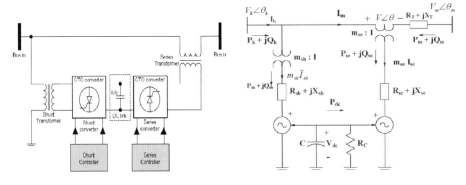

Fig. 6. Basic scheme of UPFC   **Fig. 7.** Model of UPFC

From fig.7 Power flow equations are:

$$P_k = P_{sh} + \sum \{\bar{V}_k \bar{I}_m^*\} \quad ; \quad Q_k = Q_{sh} + \sum \{\bar{V}_k \bar{I}_m^*\} \tag{5}$$

$$P_m = -\sum \{\bar{V}_m \bar{I}_m^*\} \quad ; \quad Q_m = -\sum \{\bar{V}_m \bar{I}_m^*\} \tag{6}$$

The power P_{sh} and Q_{sh} absorbed by the shunt side are refered to equation (6).

3 Test System

A 14-bus test system as shown in Fig. 8 is used for voltage stability studies. The test system consists of five generators and eleven PQ bus (or load bus). The simulation uses PSAT simulation software [11]. Using continuation power flow feature of PSAT, voltage stability of the test system is investigated. The behavior of the test system with and without FACTS devices under different loading conditions is studied. The loads are defined as:

$$P_L = P_{L0}(1 + \lambda) \; ; Q_L = Q_{L0}(1 + \lambda) \tag{7}$$

Where P_{L0} & Q_{L0} are the active and reactive base loads and P_L & Q_L are the active and reactive loads at bus L for the current operating point as defined by λ. From the continuation power flow results which are shown in Fig. 9, the buses 4, 5, 9 & 14 are the critical buses. Among these buses, bus 14 has the weakest voltage profile.
Where the system Jacobian matrix become singular at λ_{max}=2.2739 p.u.

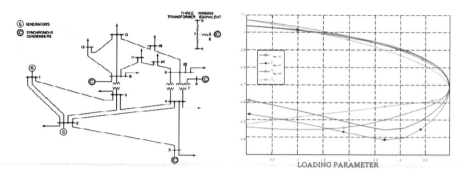

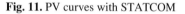

Fig. 8. The IEEE 14-bus test system   **Fig. 9.** PVcurves of test system without FACTS

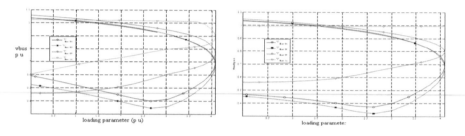

Fig. 10. PV curves with SVC   **Fig. 11.** PV curves with STATCOM

A. **SVC:** Based on collapse analysis bus 14 is targeted as the first location for an SVC. The new maximum loading level in this condition is

$$\lambda_{max}= 2.6735 p.u.$$

B. **STATCOM:** When STATCOM is connected at bus 14 we can observe from Fig. 11 that bus 14 has a flatter voltage profile. The maximum loading point is at

$$\lambda_{max} = 3.9372\ p.u.$$

C. TCSC: Next, remove the STATCOM, and insert the TCSC between bus 13 and bus 14, and then repeat to create PV curve again. The maximum loading point or critical voltage point is at $\lambda_{max} = 3.5272\ p.u.$ It can be observed that the improvement of voltage in this bus with STATCOM and SVC is more than the case with TCSC.

D. **UPFC:** A similar approach is made and the study the corresponding effects of a UPFC. The new maximum loading point in this condition is obtained

$$\lambda_{max} = 4.10391\ p.u.$$

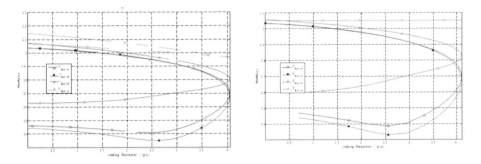

Fig. 12. PV curves with TCSC at line 13-14   **Fig. 13.** PV curves with UPFC at line 13-14

E. *Comparison of SVC, STATCOM, TCSC, and UPFC:* PV curves of base case and system with STATCOM, SVC, TCSC and UPFC are illustrated in Fig. 14. It is obvious from Fig. 14 that the MLP of the system with UPFC is highest while that with TCSC is lowest i.e., Voltage reduction is lowest in case of UPFC. The values of λ_{max} with all types of FACTS devices are compared in Table 1. From the table, it is obvious that UPFC gives the maximum loading margin compared to other devices.

UPFC provides a better voltage profile at the collapse point at the weakest bus compared to other FACTS devices. Reactive power support at the weakest bus provides better voltage profiles throughout the system.

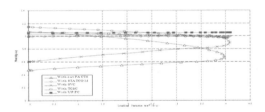

Fig. 14. PV curves of base case and system with SVC, STATCOM, TCSC and UPFC

Table 1. Maximum loading margins with various facts devices

	Base case	**SVC**	**STATCOM**	**TCSC**	**UPFC**
λ_{max}	2.2739	2.6735	3.9372	3.5272	4.1391

4   Conclusion

In this paper, voltage stability assessment of the modified IEEE 14-bus test system with SVC, STATCOM, TCSC and UPFC is studied. UPFC provides higher voltage stability margin than SVC, STATCOM and TCSC. The test system requires reactive power the most at the weakest bus, which is located in the distribution level. Introducing reactive power at this bus using UPFC can improve loading margin the most. TCSC is series compensation device, which injects reactive power through the connected line. This may not be effective when the system requires reactive power at the load level. SVC and STATCOM give slightly higher MLP and better voltage profiles compared to TCSC, since the capacity of SVC and STATCOM are higher at the collapse point than that of TCSC. It was found that these FACTS controllers significantly enhance the voltage profile and thus the loadability margin of power systems.

References

1. Blackout of 2003: Description and Responses, `http://www.pserc.wisc.edu/`
2. Kundur, P. (ed.): Voltage Stability Assessment, Procedures and Guides, technical report Final draft, IEEE/PES Power Systems Stability Subcommittee, ch. 2 (1999)
3. Caiiizares, C.A., Alvarado, F.L.: Point of Collapse and Continuation Methods for Large AD/DC Systems. IEEE Trans. Power Systems 7(1), 1–8 (1993)
4. Dobson, I., Chiang, H.D.: Towards a theory of voltage collapse in electric power systems. Systems & Control Letters 13, 253–262 (1989)
5. Cañizares, C.A., Alvarado, F.L., DeMarco, C.L., Dobson, I., Long, W.F.: Point of collapse methods applied to acldc power systems. IEEE Trans. Power Systems 7(2), 673–683 (1992)
6. Cañizares, C.A.: Power Flow and Transient Stability Models of FACTS Controllers for Voltage and Angle Stability Studies. In: Proceedings of the 2000 IEEE/PES Winter Meeting, Singapore (January 2000)
7. Cañlzares, C.A., Faur, Z.T.: Analysis SVC and TCSC Controllers in Voltage Collapse. IEEE Trans. Power Systems 14(1), 158–165 (1999)
8. Sode-Yome, A., Mithulananthan, N.: Comparison of shunt capacitor, SVC and STATCOM in static voltage stability margin enhancement. International Journal of Electrical Engineering Education, UMIST 41(3) (July 2004)
9. Kazemi, A., Vahidinasab, V., Mosallanejad, A.: Study of STATCOM and UPFC Controllers for Voltage Stability Evaluated by Saddle-Node Bifurcation Analysis. In: First International Power and Energy Coference, PECon/IEEE, Malaysia (November 2006)
10. Boonpirom, N., Paitoonwattanakij, K.: Static voltage stability enhancement using FACTS. In: The 7th International Power Engineering Conference, IPEC/IEEE (2005)
11. Milano, F.: Power System Analysis Toolbox, Version 1.3.4, Software and Documentation, July 14 (2005)

Torque Ripple Minimization of Permanent Magnet Brushless DC Motor Using Genetic Algorithm

E. Kaliappan[1] and C. Sharmeela[2]

[1] Research Scholar, Anna University, Chennai
[2] Senior Lecturer, A.C College of Engineering, Anna University

Abstract. Permanent Magnet Brushless motor DC (PMBLDC) motor is rapidly gaining popularity and are widely used in industries such as aerospace, consumer, medical, industries, automation equipment and instrumentation because of their important characteristic like high power density, Torque-inertia ratio, small size, higher efficiency. One main problem in the PMBLDC motor is the torque ripple which causes undesirable acoustic noise and vibration which affects the overall performance of the machine. The proposed work aims at minimization of torque ripple in PMBLDC motor using Genetic Algorithm (GA). By using L-C Filter ripple is minimized and PID Controller is tuned using GA.

Keywords: Permanent Magnet Brushless motor, Genetic Algorithm, Torque ripple.

1 Introduction

One main problem with PMBLDC motor is the torque ripple which affects the overall performance of the machine [1]. The cause of such unexpected behavior is a serious concern for machine designers, especially in applications where torque ripple is critical. Genetic Algorithm (GA) is search procedures based on mechanics of natural selection [2][3][4]. The objective of GA is to find an optimal solution to a multi-objective problem. We start out with a randomly selected first generation. Every string in this generation is evaluated according to its quality, and a fitness value is assigned. With a certain probability, genes are mutated before all solutions are evaluated again. This procedure is repeated until a maximum number of generations are reached.

2 Harmonics and Torque Ripple Minimization Using L-C Filter

The BLDCM is energized by the three phase inverter through an inductor - capacitor filter for reducing the high frequency component. The capacitor voltage value has to be selected in such a way that it can charge and discharge in an effective manner to reduce the high frequency component. The inductor present in series with each phase will reduce the commutation current pulsation and thereby reducing the jerk produced by commutation effects. The inverter voltage for the motor is filtered by the filter circuit provided, which minimizes the high frequency switching voltage ripple component [5][6][7]. The LC filter acts as a low pass filtering circuit minimizes harmonics in the

V. V Das, J. Stephen, and N. Thankachan et al. (Eds.): PEIE 2010, CCIS 102, pp. 53–55, 2010.
© Springer-Verlag Berlin Heidelberg 2010

supply voltage to the motor and the series inductance opposes the sudden changes in
the current due to electronic commutation and thereby reduces the torque ripple[8].

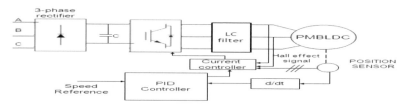

Fig. 1. Basic block diagram of PMBLDC Motor drive with L-C Filter

The basic block diagram of GA tuned PMBLDC motor drive using LC filter is
shown in Fig. 1. The L and C values are tuned using GA.To design the reactive elements present in the filter, it is assumed that the capacitor which is connected across
the load is large enough to charge and discharge, hence the capacitor voltage may be
considered to be nearly constant. Table 1 gives the GA parameters.

Table 1. GA Parameter

Crossover Probability	0.8
Mutation Probability	0.08
Generation Numbers	10

3 Simulation Results

In order to prove the superiority of the proposed method, a performance comparison
with conventional fuzzy logic has been provided. Simulated results (Fig. 2 and 3)
show a better control performance than that of the conventional method.. Therefore, a
simple implementation but a high control performance can be obtained with reduced
torque ripple of about 33.385% is obtained. The unique feature of this paper is that
GA based filter design is simple.

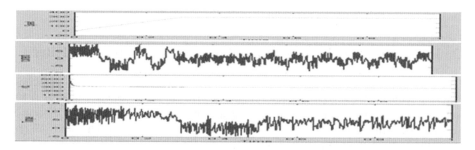

Fig. 2. Simulation results without GA: Electromagnetic torque, Rotor speed, Stator current,
Voltage

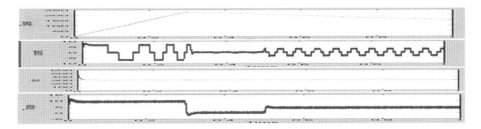

Fig. 3. Simulation results with GA: Electromagnetic torque, Rotor speed, Stator current, Voltage

4 Conclusion

From the simulated results it is evident that the harmonics components at the switching frequency and multiples of switching frequency are reduce by the filter. From the experimental results, it is found that more than half of the harmonics components are reduced with filter. The current waveforms are smoothened by the filter during the operation and the commutation frequency harmonics minimized and thereby the torque ripple is reduced. The designed PID with GA has much faster response than response of the classical method in terms of the rise time and the settling time than the conventional method.

References

1. Miller, T.J.E. (ed.): Brushless Permanent Magnet and Reluctance Drives, Clarendon, Oxford (1989); Bose, B.K.: Modern power electronics and AC drives. Prentice Hall, New Delhi
2. David, I., Goldberg, E.: Genetic Algorithms in search, optimization and machine learning. Addison-Wesley publications, Reading (1993)
3. Jeon, Y.S., Mok, H.S., Choe, G.H., Kim, D.K., Ryu, J.S.: A New Simulation Model of BLDC Motor With Real Back EMF Waveform. In: The 7th Workshop on Computers in Power Electronics, COMPEL 2000, pp. 217–220 (July 2000)
4. Hao, L., Toliyat, H.A.: BLDC Motor Full Speed Range Operation Including the Flux – Weakening Region. In: 38th IAS Annual Meeting. Conference, Record of the Industry Applications Conference, vol. 1, pp. 618–624 (October 2003)
5. Pillay, P., Krishnan, R.: Modeling, simulation, and analysis of permanent-magnet motor drives, part II: The brushless dc motor drive. IEEE Trans. Ind. Appl. IA-25(2), 274–279 (1989)
6. Bianchi, N., Bolognani, S.: Design optimization of electric motors by genetic algorithm. IEE Proceedings on Electric Power Application 145(6) (September 1998)
7. Ishikawa, T.: A method of reducing ripple torque in permanent magnet motors without skewing. IEEE Trans. Magn. 29(2), 2028–2031 (1993)
8. Kumar, P., Bauer, P.: Delft University of Technology, Mekelweg 4, 2628CD Delft, The Netherlands MULTI-OBJECTIVE optimization of BLDC motor. In: 10th International Symposium on Mechatronics, Mechatronika 2007, Trenčianske Teplice, Slovakia, June 6-8 (2007)

Residential-Scale Solar/Pico-Hydel/Wind Based Hybrid Energy System for Remote Area Electrification

S. Kumarvel[1] and S. Ashok[2]

[1] Assistant Professor, National Institute of Technology, Calicut, Kerala, India
kumaravel_s@nitc.ac.in
[2] Professor, National Institute of Technology, Calicut, Kerala, India

Abstract. This paper reports an investigation on the economic aspects of stand-alone Solar/Pico-Hydro/Wind Hybrid Energy System (HES) for typical unelectrified houses in a remote area at Pathanpara, Kannur (Dist), Kerala India. Mathematical model of wind/solar/hydel system is developed and it is simulated in MATLAB/SIMULINK platform. A detailed survey is conducted to assess the potential of hydel, solar, wind energy and electricity demand of a typical house at Pathanpara. Various parameters of commercially available renewable generators are collected and performance is evaluated in the developed simulation model in MATLAB. The optimization for unit sizing and source selection is performed for the collected data from the survey using HOMER. The economic analysis of the proposed Hybrid Energy System is carried out and the results are presented in this paper.

Keywords: Hybrid Energy System, Rural Electrification, Unit sizing, Renewable Energy, Alternative Energy.

1 Introduction

Renewable energy is a non-depleting, environment friendly and potential source of alternative energy options. The continuous decline of costs for renewable energy technology and establishment of matured expertise have increased the widespread utilization of renewable energy. However, the renewable energy sources influenced by natural conditions are intermittent and also site dependent. Therefore, it is difficult to accomplish reliable energy supply only by one source. In order to achieve high energy availability and reliability, it is necessary to interconnect two or more renewable energy sources together as renewable Hybrid Energy Systems. It is also an excellent solution for power generation in rural areas where the grid extension is difficult and uneconomical [1-7]. Design and simulation of various hybrid systems are discussed in [8-12]. HOMER package is used to perform the optimization of unit sizing and source selection.

2 System Description

The renewable sources such as wind, solar and hydel are taken as the primary sources and battery bank is used as a backup and storage system. This system can be considered

V. V Das, J. Stephen, and N. Thankachan et al. (Eds.): PEIE 2010, CCIS 102, pp. 56–62, 2010.
© Springer-Verlag Berlin Heidelberg 2010

as a complete "green" power generation system because the main energy sources are all environmental friendly. Figure 1 depicts the topology of the proposed Hybrid Energy System consisting of variable speed Wind Turbine (WT) coupled to a Permanent Magnet DC Generator (PMDCG), solar PV module, Pico-Hydel turbine coupled with PMDCG, battery storage unit, power conditioning circuit, AC, DC bus bar and Load. Renewable energy sources are integrated in a common DC bus line through multiple input DC/DC converter.

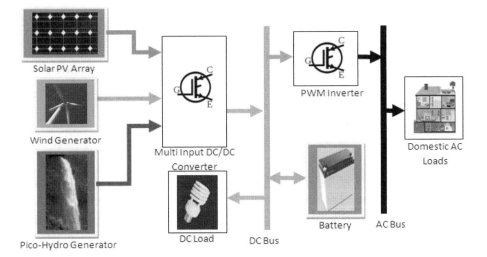

Fig. 1. Proposed system configuration

So, power conditioning and integration is simpler than the integration of these sources in AC bus bar. It is possible to utilize the power available with the renewable generator under certain level. A PWM voltage source inverter is employed to convert the DC power into 440V, 50 Hz AC.

3 Optimization Model and Simulation of the Proposed System

The objective of the optimization model is to optimize the availability of energy to the loads according to their levels of priority. It is also proposed to maintain a fair level of energy storage to meet peak load along with or without wind, PV array and hydel sources. It is desired to minimize dumped energy, $Q_{dump}(t)$. The dumped energy is the excess energy or energy which cannot be utilized by the loads.

The objective function is to maximize

$$\sum_{t=1}^{24}\left\{\sum_{i} P_i I_i(t) - Q_{dump}(t)\right\}$$ (1)

With $I_i(t) \geq 0$

Where, t is hour of a particular day t = 1,2, ...24

i is type of primary and deferrable loads

P_i is demand of load i at time t in kW

$I_i(t)$ is the function of time for the load i

Load Constraints: The energy distribution from the energy devices at period t to each load i is given as follows:

$$Q_{P,i}(t)+Q_{W,i}(t)+Q_{H,i}(t)+Q_{B,i}(t)= I_i(t)P_i \qquad (2)$$

Where $Q_{P,i}(t),Q_{W,i}(t),Q_{H,i}(t),Q_{B,i}(t)$ are the energy supplied by PV, Wind, Hydel and Battery respectively.

PV Array constraints: $E_p(t)$ is the sum of the energy supplied by the PV array to the loads and to the battery bank at hour t,

$$Q_{P,B}(t)+\left(\sum_i Q_{P,i}(t)\right)+Q_{P,R}(t)= E_P(t) \qquad (3)$$

Where $Q_{P,R}(t)$ is the energy dumped by the PV array

$Q_{P,B}(t)$ is the energy supplied by the PV array to the battery bank

Since energy generated by the PV system varies with insolation, the available array energy $E_p(t)$ at any particular time is given by

$$E_p(t)= VS(t) \qquad (4)$$

Where V is the capacity of PV array

S(t) is the insolation index

Wind energy system constraints: $E_W(t)$ is the sum of the energy supplied by the wind energy system to the loads and battery bank at hour t,

$$Q_{W,B}(t)+\left(\sum_i Q_{p,i}(t)\right)+Q_{W,R}(t)= E_W(t) \qquad (5)$$

Where, $Q_{W,R}(t)$ is the dumped energy by the wind energy system.

$Q_{W,B}(t)$ is the energy supplied by the wind energy system to battery bank.

Hydel energy system constrains: $E_H(t)$ is the sum of the energy supplied by the wind energy system to the loads and battery bank at hour t,

$$Q_{H,B}(t)+\left(\sum_i Q_{p,i}(t)\right)+Q_{H,R}(t)= E_H(t) \qquad (6)$$

Where, $Q_{H,R}(t)$ is the dumped energy by the hydel energy system.

$Q_{H,B}(t)$ is the energy supplied by the hydel energy system to battery bank.

Battery bank constraints: The battery serves as an energy source entity when discharging and as a load when charging. The net energy balance to the battery determines its State-of-Charge, (SOC) the state of charge is expressed as follows

$$Q_B SOC(t) = Q_B SOC(t-1) + (Q_P(t) + Q_G(t) + Q_W(t)) - \sum_i Q_{B,i}(t) \tag{7}$$

Where, Q_B is the capacity of the battery bank

The battery has to be protected against overcharging, therefore the charge level at *(t-1)* plus the influx of energy from the PV, wind and gasifier at period *(t-1)* should not exceed the capacity of the battery.

Mathematically,

$$Q_B \geq Q_B SOC(t-1) + Q_P(t) + Q_G(t) + Q_W(t) \tag{8}$$

The excessive power available with renewable source will become the unutilized power when the battery is fully charged.

A generalized mathematical model of the proposed system is developed. Developed mathematical model is simulated in MATLAB/SIMULINK and the performances are verified. Variable parameters of commercially available renewable sources based electrical generators such as solar, wind and pico-hydel are collected. These variables are validated using the developed model in MATLAB/ SIMULINK platform. Figure 2 shows the load profile and potentials of solar, wind and hydel for year 2009 at Pathanpara. Load curve is developed based on the nature, number and power of appliances owned by rural households, as well as their operation periods. From the results of this survey, it is observed that the daily energy demand of a household that uses electricity

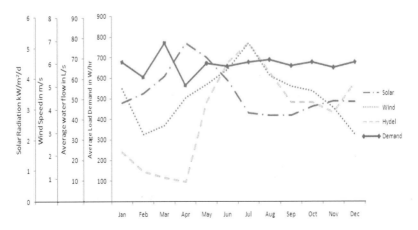

Fig. 2. Load profile, solar, wind and hydel potential at Pathanpara for a day

for lighting, refrigeration, television, etc. is 23.98 kWh/day. The global horizontal solar radiation of Pathanpara is measured at hourly intervals from 6:00 to 18.00. It is found that the average monthly insolation of Pathanpara on the horizontal plane is in the range 2.4–5.8 kWh/m^2/day. Solar radiation is maximum during April month about 4.9 kWh/m^2/day and minimum during August about 2.65 kWh/m^2/day.

The village has enough wind potential, since in several locations the annual mean wind speed exceeds 4.93 m/s, at 15m height. Wind speeds are generally higher in monsoon months (May-Aug.) as compared to other months. This clearly reflects that a WECS would produce appreciably more energy during monsoon months as compared to the other months. The data also shows that there is considerable variation of monthly average wind speed for the same month. The study area has adequate stream flow available 8-10 months in a year frequently. Maximum water flow is 80 L/s during July. The height between the turbine point and storage tank is 22 m.

4   Optimization of Unit Sizing and Source Selection

The developed mathematical model is formulated with the specified constraints and optimization is carried out for unit sizing and source selection of the proposed system in HOMER software package which is developed by NREL, USA for Hybrid Energy System. Table 1 list the optimal unit size, capital cost and Cost of Energy (CoE), etc., of solar PV module, wind generator, hydel turbine, battery and converter obtained from the simulation. The proposed Hybrid Energy System requires a capital cost of Rs. 4.71 lacks.

Table 1. Optimal unit size, capital cost and cost of energy

HES Component	Installed Capacity	Electricity Production in kWh/year	CoE of HES in Rs/kWh
Solar PV	1 kW	1427	
Wind	1 kW	1341	
Pico-Hydro	3 kW	17072	
Battery	200 Ah	Not Applicable (NA)	4.348
Converter	3 kW	NA	
Miscellaneous	NA	NA	

Estimated CoE is Rs. 4.348 per unit which is cheaper than Diesel Generator (DG), stand-alone solar PV and WECS. CoE of various combination of HES is shown in figure 3. Pico-Hydel generation alone is the best configuration to use. But the reliability of electricity is poor during February-May.

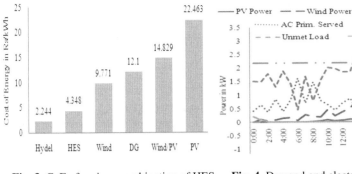

Fig. 3. CoE of various combination of HES

Fig. 4. Demand and electricity generation for a typical day

Major part of the demand is met by hydel system. Demand, generated electricity from the source, excess and unmet energy of the proposed HES for a typical day is shown in figure 4. Negative part of Battery input power curve indicates the charging mode. From the figure it is observed that the contribution of battery is much essential during peak load hours. It is acting as source during this interval.

5   Conclusions

Solar/Pico-Hydel/Wind HES is proposed to meet the demand of typical unelectrified houses situated in the rural area Pathanpara, Kannur, Kerala. An optimization model is developed for unit sizing and source selection in HOMER. Each source is complimentary to other source in the proposed Hybrid Energy System. Cost analysis proves the feasibility of the proposed Hybrid Energy System to meet the demand of rural areas. The intermittent nature renewable energy sources are integrated to DC bus in the proposed system to eliminate the stability and power quality constrains. Hydel system is involved as one of the source in HES. So this can be utilized for pumped storage which can further minimize the size of the battery. This will further reduce the Cost of Energy.

References

1. Elhadidy, M.A., Shaahid, S.M.: Promoting applications of hybrid (wind + photovoltaic + diesel + battery) power systems in hot regions. Renewable Energy 29, 517–528 (2003)
2. Celik, A.N.: Techno-economic analysis of autonomous PV-wind hybrid energy systems using different sizing methods. Energy Conversion and Management 44, 1951–1968 (2003)
3. Celik, A.N.: Optimization and techno-economic analysis of autonomous photovoltaic-wind hybrid energy systems in comparison to single photovoltaic and wind systems. Conversion and Management 43, 2453–2468 (2002)
4. Rana, S., Chandra, R., Singh, S.P., Sodha, M.S.: Optimal Mix of Renewable Energy Resources to Meet the Electrical Energy Demand in Villages of Madhya Pradesh. Energy Conversion and Management 39(3/4), 203–216 (1998)

5. Gavanidou, E.S., Bakirtzis, A.G.: Design of a stand-alone system with renewable energy sources using trade off methods. IEEE Trans. on Energy Conversion 7(1), 42–48 (1992)
6. Ashok, S.: Optimized model for community-based hybrid energy system. Renewable Energy 32, 1155–1164 (2007)
7. Kellogg, W.D., Nehrir, M.H., Venkataramanan, G., Gerez, V.: Generation Unit Sizing and Cost Analysis for Stand-Alone Wind, Photovoltaic, and Hybrid Wind/PV Systems. IEEE Transactions on Energy Conversion 13(1) (1998)
8. Nayar, C.V., Lawrance, W.B., Phillips, S.J.: Solar/Wind/Diesel Hybrid Energy Systems for Remote Areas. In: Proceedings of the 24th Intersociety Energy Conversion Engineering Conference, pp. 2029–2034 (1989)
9. Elhadidy, M.A., Shaahid, S.M.: Feasibility of hybrid (wind + solar) power systems for Dhahran Saudi Arabia. Renewable Energy 16, 970–976 (1999)
10. Nfah, E.M., Ngundam, J.M.: Feasibility of pico-hydro and photovoltaic hybrid power systems for remote villages in Cameroon. Renewable Energy 34, 1445–1450 (2009)
11. Elhadidy, M.A., Shaahid, S.M.: Optimal sizing of battery storage for hybrid (wind+diesel) power systems. Renew Energy 18, 77–86 (1999)
12. Balamurugan, P., Ashok, S., Jose, T.L.: Optimal scheduling and operation of Solar/wind/PV/biomass based hybrid system for rural areas. International Journal of Energy Technology and Policy 7(1), 113–126 (2009)

Designing CDMA Modem in FPGA Based on DSSS

Amit Tripathi and M.S. Korde

Department of Electronics Engg
Shri Ramdeobaba Kamla Nehru Engineering College
R.T.M. Nagpur University, Nagpur, India-440013
amit_tp25@yahoo.com, mridula_korde@yahoo.com

Abstract. In a DS-SS system, each user is assigned a unique code sequence (PN-Sequence) that allows the user to spread the information signal across the assigned frequency band. Signals from the various users are separated at the receiver by cross correlation of the received signal with each of the possible user code sequences. Possible narrow band interference is also suppressed in this process. Because of its advantages, it is used in CDMA systems to assign a unique code to every user. This paper describes the design of CDMA modem in FPGA based on DSSS. 8051 microcontroller & FPGA were linked with rf transmitter/receiver, a acknowledgement was being sent to FPGA once the bit was transmitted/receive by the 8051 microcontroller. At the receiver output of 8051 microcontroller was compared with the threshold levels using a comparator and this provides binary output which is the actually transmitted sequence.

Keywords: Code Division Multiple Access (CDMA), Direct Sequence Spread Spectrum (DSSS), Pseudo Random (PN) Sequence, 8051 microcontroller, Field Programmable gate array (FPGA), Radio Frequence (RF) Transmitter/Receiver.

1 Introduction

Direct Sequence Spread Spectrum (DSSS) as the name suggests uses a Pseudo Random (PN) Sequence to generate the output bit pattern based on modulo-2 addition between the input sequence and the PN Sequence. In DSSS each user is assigned a unique code sequence (which is the PN Sequence) that allows the user to spread the information signal across the assigned frequency band[1][2].

Signals from the various users are separated at the receiver by cross correlation of the received signal with each of the possible user code sequences. Possible narrow band interference is also suppressed in this process. By designing these code sequences to have relatively small cross-correlation, the cross-talk inherent in the demodulation of the signals received from multiple transmitters is minimized[6].

2 CDMA

Code Division Multiple Access is a form of a DSSS system. This modulation transforms an information bearing signal into a transmission signal with a much larger

V. V Das, J. Stephen, and N. Thankachan et al. (Eds.): PEIE 2010, CCIS 102, pp. 63–68, 2010.
© Springer-Verlag Berlin Heidelberg 2010

bandwidth. This transformation is achieved by encoding the information signal with a code signal that is independent of the data and has much larger spectral width than the data[3].

As the name suggests CDMA (Code Division Multiple Access) allows users to share the same frequency band and still be able to communicate securely. This is possible due to the fact that in CDMA every user is assigned is unique code which helps in decoding only that signal which is meant for the user and remaining signals are decoded in error which are garbage values for the given receiver.

For a DSSS based CDMA system the code assigned to the user is the PN sequence. The length of this indicates the amount of bandwidth and the amount of security the system can provide to the communication system[4].

3 PN Sequence Generator

A PN Sequence generator is a device which is responsible for generating various random code sequences. These random code sequences are then used for coding and decoding the message sequence. Different logic can be applied to generate a random PN sequences in a real time scenario and assigning each one of them to a different system.

The same PN sequence generator is used at both the transmitter and the receiver which ensures that the exactly same PN sequence is used for both encoding and decoding the message bits[1][2].

4 CDMA Using DS-SS

In a DS-SS system, each user is assigned a unique code sequence that allows the user to spread the information signal across the assigned frequency band. Signals from the various users are separated at the receiver by cross correlation of the received signal with each of the possible user code sequences. Possible narrow band interference is also suppressed in this process. By designing these code sequences to have relatively small cross-correlation, the cross-talk inherent in the demodulation of the signals received from multiple transmitters is minimize. This multiple access method is CDMA, which is a form of a DSSS system[4]. This modulation transforms an information bearing signal into a transmission signal with a much larger bandwidth. This transformation is achieved by encoding the information signal with a code signal that is independent of the data and has much larger spectral width than the data signal. This spreads the original signal power over a much broader bandwidth, resulting in a lower power density. The ratio of transmitted bandwidth to information bandwidth is called the processing gain Gp of the DS-SS system: $Gp = Bt/Bi$, where Bt is the transmission bandwidth and Bi is the bandwidth of the information bearing signal. In DS-SS transmitter the data is spread by multiplying with a pseudorandom noise (PN) sequence. A PN sequence is a binary sequence that exhibits randomness properties but has a finite length and is therefore deterministic. They are used to implement synchronization and uniquely code individual user signals across the transmission interface. PN generators are based on Linear Feedback Shift Registers (LFSR)[5].

A DS-SS receiver is based on a correlator, which utilizes correlation properties of the PN codes. The correlators attempt to match the incoming received signal with each of the candidate prototype waveforms (PN sequences) known a prior to the receiver[1][2]. Since we deal with the discrete signals in practice, the discrete form of the correlation of two discrete signals is given as

$$r_{xy}(k) = \sum_{n=0}^{N-1} x(n)\,y(k+n) \tag{1}$$

5 DS-CDMA System

5.1 Transmitter

The transmitter as shown in fig.1 has clock divider which divides the high frequency clock for the Data latch and the PN Code generator to work in synchronization with each other. The data latch is used to latch the input data and provide it bit by bit for modulo-2 addition to the modulo-2adder. PN Code Generator block generates a random PN sequence unique for every message data input. It provides the PN Code bit-by-bit to the modulo-2 adder for addition with the input bit sequence.Modulo-2 Adder is actually a XORing circuit which performs the addition of the input bit sequence with the PN Sequence[1][2].

At the transmitter side, the generated sequence at the FPGA which is to be transmitted was given in parallel to the 8051 microcontroller as shown in fig.2 in 8 bit size when a signal regarding data sequence transmission was enabled & given to the 8051 microcontroller[7]. The output from the 8051 microcontroller was transmitted serially one bit at a time using rf transmitter & an acknowledgement regarding transmitted data was given to the FPGA.

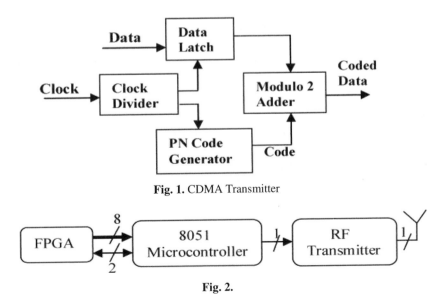

Fig. 1. CDMA Transmitter

Fig. 2.

5.2 Receiver

The receiver has Multiplier Accumulator Circuit (MAC) which performs successive addition of the input data modulo-2 added with the PN sequence which was used at the transmitter. The output of this MAC is given to the comparator. PN Code Generator block is same as used in the DSSS transmitter. Threshold block is used to provide a threshold level to the incoming input bits. Setting of thresholds is done to get an exact output from an approximate output. Hence this block should be pre configured with the transmitter in order to get an approximately exact received output. The comparator compares the output of MAC with the threshold levels set at the Threshold Device.

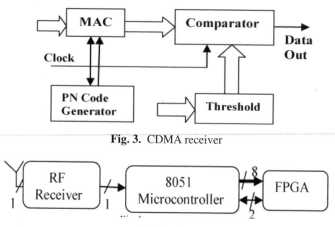

Fig. 3. CDMA receiver

Fig. 4.

At the receiver side, the received signal from the RF receiver was applied to the 8051 microcontroller as shown in fig.4 where it is stored & applied in parallel in 8 bit size to the FPGA when signal from 8051 microcontroller to FPGA is enable, & an acknowledgement regarding received data was given to the 8051 microcontroller[7]. The received data at FPGA was then compared using a comparator and provides binary output which is the actually transmitted sequence[1][2].

6   Limitation of DS-CDMA Based Modem

The main problem with DS-CDMA systems is the Near- Far effect. If there are more than one users active, the transmitted power of non-reference users is suppressed by a factor dependent on the (partial) cross correlation between the code of the reference user and the code of a non reference user. However when a non- reference user is closer to the receiver then the reference-user, it is possible that the interference caused by this non- reference user(However suppressed) has more power then the reference user. Now only the non-reference user will be received, this property is called the near-far effect.

7 Result

The simulation of the entire DSSS based CDMA system has been implemented using FPGA, which provides for input of real time audio signals. The evaluation of signal values was performed using a program written in VHDL. The transmitted signal was seen to be successfully reproduced at the receiver. Our methods are demonstrated through extensive synthesis experiments using the Xilinx ISE 9.1i FPGA device family.

The transmitter output waveform was as shown in fig.7,generated by XORing of latched input with the PN sequence as shown in fig.5 when a clock pulse from the clock divider output was applied for synchronizing the latched inputs & PN sequence.

The receiver output waveform was as shown in fig.8,generated by XORing of received sequence with the same PN sequence which was used at the transmitter. The received output sequence was same as the applied input sequence which was compared using a comparator.

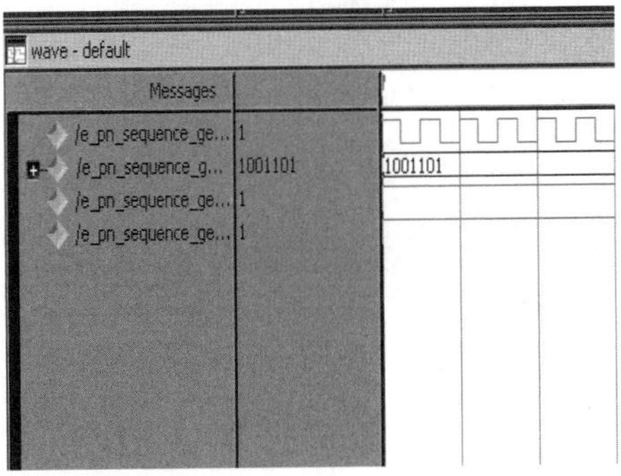

Fig. 5. PN Sequence Output Waveform

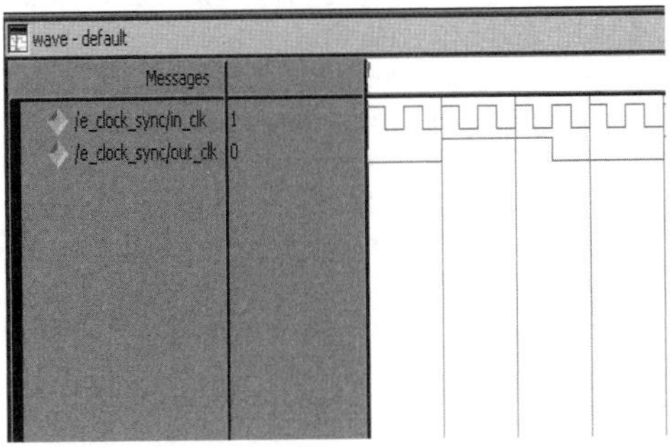

Fig. 6. Clock Divider Output Waveform

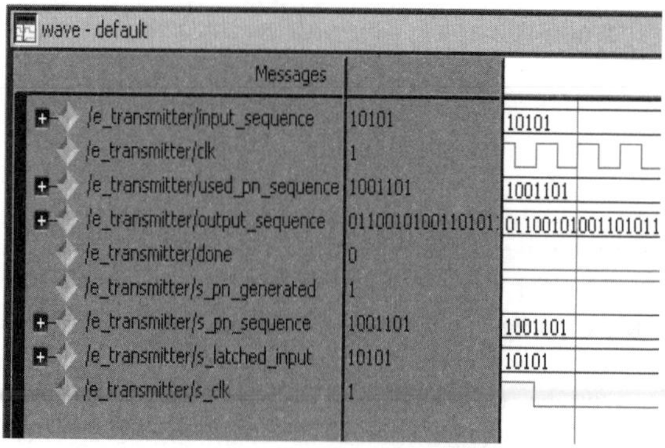

Fig. 7. CDMA Transmitter Output Waveform

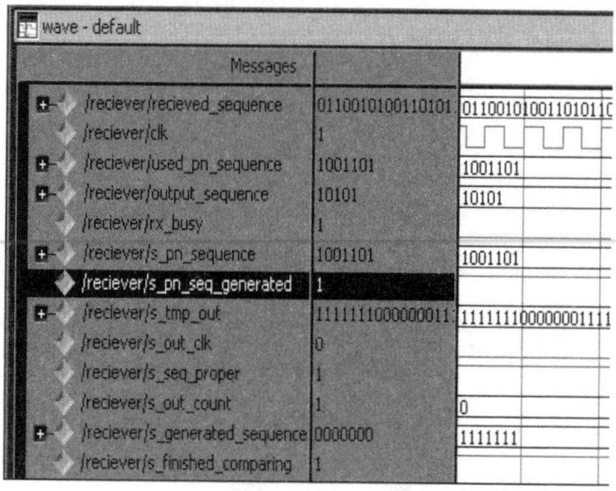

Fig. 8. Receiver output Waveform

References

1. Haykin, S.: Digital Communication. Wiley India Pvt. Ltd., Chichester (2006)
2. Proakis, J.G.: Digital Communication, 4th edn. McGraw-hill, New York
3. Taub, H., Schillingn, D.L.: 2nd edn. Tata McGraw-Hill
4. Khairnar, K., Nema, S.: Comparison of Multi-User detectors of DSCDMA System. Transactions on Engineering, computing and Technology 10 (December 2005) ISSN 1305- 5313
5. Kocian, A., Fluery, B.H.: EM–based joint data detection and channel estimation of DS–CDMA signals. IEEE Trans. Commun. 51(10), 1709–1720 (2003)
6. Duel-Hallen, A.: A family of multiuser decision – feedback detectors for asynchronous code-divison multiple access channels. IEEE Trans. Comm. 43(2-4), 421–434 (1995)
7. Mazidi, M.A.: The 8051 Microcontroller and Embedded Systems, 2nd edn. Pearson, Prentice Hall, London (2006)

Voltage Clamped DC-DC Converter with Reduced Reverse Recovery Current and Switch Voltage Stress

P. Hari Krishna Prasad[1] and Venu Gopala Rao Mannam[2]

[1] Prof. & HOD, EEE, Adam's Engineering College, Paloncha 507115, Khammam Dist, A.P.
[2] Dr.Venu Gopala Rao Mannam, Prof.& BOS Chairman, Dept. of EEE, KL University, A.P.

Abstract. Rectifier reverse-recovery problems cause a significant efficiency reduction as well as severe electromagnetic interference (EMI) in continuous-current-mode (CCM) boost converters. To alleviate these problems, this paper presents a simple and effective solution that involves shifting the original rectifier current to a new branch, which consists of a rectifier and a coupled winding of the boost inductor. A high-efficiency clamped voltage dc–dc converter with reduced reverse-recovery current and switch-voltage stress. In the circuit topology, it is designed by way of the combination of inductor and transformer to increase the corresponding voltage gain. Moreover, one additional inductor provides the reverse-current path of the transformer to enhance the utility rate of magnetic core. In addition, the voltage-clamped technology is used to reduce the switch-voltage stress.

I Introduction

In recent years, dc–dc converters with steep voltage ratio are usually required in many industrial applications, e.g., the front-end stage for clean energy sources, the dc backup energy system for an uninterruptible power supply (UPS), high intensity discharge (HID) lamps for automobile headlamps, and the telecommunication industry [1]-[3]. The conventional boost converters cannot provide such a high dc-voltage ratio due to the losses associated with the inductor, filter capacitor, main switch, and output diode. Even for an extreme duty cycle, it will result in serious reverse-recovery problems and increase the rating of the output diode. As a result, the conversion efficiency is degraded. In order to increase the conversion efficiency and voltage gain, many modified boost-converter topologies have been investigated in the past decade.[4],[5].

Although voltage-clamped techniques are manipulated in the converter design to overcome the severe reverse-recovery problem of the output diode in high-level voltage applications, there still exist overlarge switch-voltage stresses, and the voltage gain is limited by the turn-ON time of the auxiliary switch.[4],[5] presented a boost soft-single-switch converter, which has only one single active switch is able to operate with soft switching in a pulse width modulation (PWM) way without high voltage and current stresses.

The aim of this paper is to design a high-efficiency voltage clamped dc–dc converter with reduced reverse-recovery current and switch-voltage stress to provide a stable constant dc voltage. To achieve this goal, the manipulation of inductor and

V. V Das, J. Stephen, and N. Thankachan et al. (Eds.): PEIE 2010, CCIS 102, pp. 69 – 73, 2010.
© Springer-Verlag Berlin Heidelberg 2010

transformer is adopted to increase the voltage gain and to enhance the utility rate of the magnetic core. Moreover, the voltage-clamped technology is used for reducing the switch voltage stress and solving the reverse-recovery problem.

2   Converter Design and Analysis

A newly designed converter topology contains four parts including a dc-input circuit, a primary-side circuit, a secondary-side circuit and a dc-output circuit. C_s and C_c are the balanced capacitor and clamped capacitor in the secondary-side circuit. The equivalent circuit and state definition of the newly designed converter is depicted in Fig. 1 , where the transformer is modeled as an ideal transformer with a secondary leakage inductor (L_k). The turn's ratio of this ideal transformer is define

$$n = N_2/N_1 \tag{1}$$

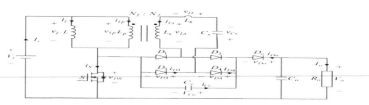

Fig. 1. Equivalent circuit

The additional inductor (L) is located in parallel with the primary side of the transformer. The clamped capacitor Cc is assumed to be large enough to be viewed as a constant voltage source, V_{Cc} . The conductive voltage drops of the main switch (S) and all diodes (D_1, D_2, D_3, D_4, and D_o) are neglected to simplify the circuit analyses, and the detailed operation stages are described as follows.

A.   Mode 1 (t_0 - t_1) [Fig. 2(a)]

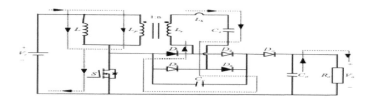

B.   Mode 2 (t_1 - t_2) [Fig. 2(b)]

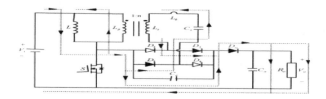

At time t = t_0, the main switch (S) is turned ON. At the same time, the diodes (D_1 and D_4) become conducted, and other diodes (D_2, D_3, and D_o) are reverse biased. The additional inductor (L) and clamped capacitor (C_c) are linearly charged by the input-voltage source (V_i) through the transformer. Applying Kirchhoff's law [4], the voltages of v_L, v_{Lp}, v_{Ls}, and v_{Lk} during this period can be expressed as

$$v_L = v_{Lp} = V_i \tag{2}$$
$$v_{Ls} = n\, V_i \tag{3}$$
$$v_{Lk} = V_{Cc} - n\, V_i - v_{Cs}. \tag{4}$$

According to (2)–(4), the rate of change of the additional inductor current (i_L), the primary-side current (i_{Lp}), and the secondary-side current (i_{Ls}) of the transformer can be represented

$$di_L/dt = V \tag{5}$$
$$di_{Lp}/dt = (V_{Cc} - nV_i - v_{Cs})/L_k + V_i \tag{6}$$
$$di_{Ls}/dt = (V_{Cc} - nV_i - v_{Cs})/L \tag{7}$$

C.   Mode 2 (t_1 - t_2) [Fig. 2(c)]

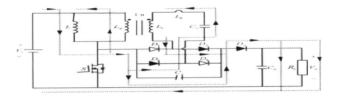

At time t = t_1, the main switch (S) is turned OFF. At this time, the diodes (D_2, D_3, and D_o) become forward biased to start conducting, and other diodes (D_1 and D_4) are reverse biased. The stored energy of the additional inductor (L) and clamped capacitor (C_c) in Mode 1 is released to output loads. Moreover, the transformer can be operated at four quadrants to enhance the utility rate of the magnetic core and to keep the clamped voltage (V_{Cc}), since the additional inductor (L) supplies energy to the output terminal by way of the transformer. Applying Kirchhoff's law [4], the voltage and current relations of each element during this mode can be described by

$$v_L = v_{Lp} = V_i + V_{Cc} - V_o \tag{8}$$
$$v_{Ls} = n\,(V_i + V_{Cc} - V_o) \tag{9}$$
$$v_Lk = -V_{Cc} - v_{Cs} - n\,(V_i + V_{Cc} - V_o) \tag{10}$$
$$v_{DS} = V_i - V_L = V_o - V_{Cc} < V_o \tag{11}$$
$$i_{Do} = i_L + i_{Lp} = i_{Cc} - i_{Ls} \tag{12}$$

where i_{Do} is the current of the output diode D_o; i_{Cc} is the current of the clamped capacitor C_c. According to (11), the cutoff voltage of the main switch (S) is clamped at V_o - V_{Cc}. Moreover, the main switch (S) with low-voltage-rated capacity can be selected since the switch-voltage stress (v_{DS}) is smaller than the output voltage (V_o). The selection of a low-voltage rated device with lower $R_{DS(ON)}$ is useful for improving the conversion efficiency. Referring to (8)–(10), the rate of change of i_L, i_{Lp} and i_{Ls} is given by

$$di_L/dt = (V_i + V_{Cc} - V_o) / L \qquad (13)$$
$$di_{Lp}/dt = [-V_{Cc} - v_{Cs} - n(V_i + V_{Cc} - V_o) / L_k] + (V_i + V_{Cc} - V_o) / L_p \qquad (14)$$
$$di_{Ls}/dt = [-V_{Cc} - v_{Cs} - n(V_i + V_{Cc} - V_o)] / L_k \qquad 15)$$

At time $t = t_2$, the residual energy of the clamped capacitor (C_c) is discharged entirely, i.e., $i_{Cc} (t_2) = 0$. Immediately, the clamped capacitor (C_c) is charged by the energy of the additional inductor (L) through the transformer, and the rate of change of the clamped-capacitor current (i_{Cc}) where d is the duty cycle of the main switch (S). Continuously, the main switch (S) is turned ON at time $t = t_4$ to begin the next switching cycle. Since the voltage difference may be caused by the secondary inductor of the transformer, as $d \neq 0.5$, the major function of the balanced capacitor (C_c) is used for keeping the cutoff voltages of the rectifier diodes (D_1, D_2, D_3, and D_4) balanced. Moreover, it also can avoid the overlarge current that passed through the rectifier diodes. According to the voltage gain can be tuned by regulating the turns ratio (n) in the transformer to overcome the boost-ratio limitation of the conventional converter. In addition, the switch-voltage stress (v_{DS}).

By analyzing the switch-voltage stress (v_{DS}) is not related to the dc-input voltage (V_i) and duty cycle (d) if the values of the output voltage (V_o) and the turns ratio (n) are fixed. Thus, it can ensure that the sustainable voltage of the main switch (S) is constant. As long as the dc-input voltage is not higher than the rated voltage of the main switch, the high-efficiency voltage clamped dc–dc converter can be applied well to the low-voltage power sources even with large voltage variations, e.g., fuel cell, solar cell, etc.

3 Circuit and Waveforms

3.1 Simulation Circuit

A prototype of the converter circuit has been built with input voltage $V_i = 10$ V, Clamped capacitor, Cc = 6× 4.7 µF and a switching frequency of 100 **kHz.** Maximum output power at $V_O = 60V$ is 80W. The converter always operates in the continuous conduction mode.

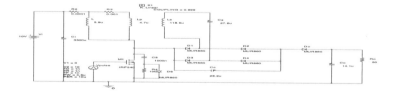

3.2 Experimental Results

OUTPUT VOLTAGE

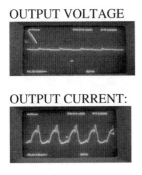

OUTPUT CURRENT:

4 Conclusion

This project has developed a voltage-clamped dc–dc converter with reduced reverse recovery current and switch-voltage stress, with a power quality of low voltage and high current. The newly designed converter circuit has the following improvements compared to the previous work.

It can select the main switch with lower sustainable voltage for alleviating the switch conduction loss due to the utilization of voltage-clamped technique. The additional inductor is used for providing the reverse current path of the transformer to raise the utility rate of the magnetic core. Additional snubber circuits for absorbing the voltage spikes in the diodes are not required to further cut down the manufacture cost.

References

1. Barbi, I., Gules, R.: Isolated dc\\\–dc converters with high-output voltage for TWTA tele-communication satellite applications. IEEE Trans. Power Electron. 18(4) (2003)
2. Abutbul, O., Gherlitz, A., Berkovich, Y., Ioinovici, A.: Step-up switching-mode converter with high voltage gain using a switched-capacitor circuit. IEEE Trans. Circuits Syst. I, Fundam. Theory Appl. 50(8) (2003)
3. Tseng, K.C., Liang, T.J.: Novel high-efficiency step-up converter. Proc. Inst. Elect. Eng.\\\—Electr. Power Appl. 151(2) (2004)
4. Jovanovic, M.M., Jang, Y.: A new soft-switched boost converter with isolated active snubber. IEEE Trans. Ind. Appl. 35(2) (1999)
5. Duarte, C.M.C., Barbi, I.: An improved family of ZVS-PWM active-clamping DC-to-DC converters. IEEE Trans. Power Electron. 17(1) (2002)

Online Monitoring of Available Transfer Capability in Deregulated Power System Using Adaptive Neuro Fuzzy Inference System

P. Gopi Krishna[1], T. Gowri Manohar[2], and G. N. Srinivas[3]

[1] Associate Professor, Dept. of EEE, Narayana Engg., College, Nellore, A.P., India
p_gopikrishna2000@yahoo.com
[2] Associate Professor, Dept. of EEE, S.V.University College of Engg., Tirupati, A.P., India
tgmanohar1973@gmail.com
[3] Associate Professor, Dept. of EEE, J.N.T.University, Hyderabad, A.P., India
gnsgns.srinivas785@gmail.com

Abstract. In this paper, a novel and an easy approach is proposed for the on-line monitoring of the Available Transfer Capability (ATC), which is a necessary, significant and challenging task in the deregulated power system. The ATC is evaluated with and without contingencies at various load conditions for different load buses, using the conventional method (Repeated Power Flow) and the proposed Adaptive Neuro Fuzzy Inference System (ANFIS). The ANFIS network is trained with the training data of the conventional method and its performance is verified with the checking data. The comparative results of both methods indicate that the trained ANFIS network is best to use in an online environment of deregulated power system, in view of its computational procedure and simplicity in adapting to original system.

Keywords: RPF, TTC, ATC, ANN, ANFIS, Contingency, Deregulated, etc.

1 Introduction

The electrical power system is continuously expanding in size and growing in complexity all over the world with the increase of population and modernization. Therefore the governments have been changing their rules and regulations by allowing the private sectors into the power generation, transmission and distribution (Deregulated Power System). The security in the deregulated power system for the load flow is less. Under this insecure environment the power system engineer has to monitor the ATC continuously in an on-line [1].

Repeated power flow [2] in the power system parlance is steady state solution of the power system network. The main information obtained from this study comprises the magnitudes and phase angles of load bus voltages, reactive powers at generator buses, real and reactive power flow on transmission lines, and other variables are specified.

Available transfer capability (ATC) [3] is the measure of the ability of interconnected electric systems to reliably transfer power from one area to another through all

V. V Das, J. Stephen, and N. Thankachan et al. (Eds.): PEIE 2010, CCIS 102, pp. 74–79, 2010.
© Springer-Verlag Berlin Heidelberg 2010

transmission lines, between those areas under specified system conditions. It is clear that ATC information is significant to the secure operation of deregulated power systems [4] as it reflects physical realities of the transmission system such as customer demand level, network paradigm, generation dispatch and transfer between neighboring systems. In order to obtain ATC, the total transfer capability (TTC) should be evaluated first where TTC is the largest flow through selected interfaces or corridors of the transmission network.

Neuro-Fuzzy hybridization [5] results in a hybrid intelligent system that synergizes artificial neural networks and fuzzy systems by combining the human-like reasoning style of fuzzy systems through the use of fuzzy sets and a linguistic model consisting of a set of IF-THEN fuzzy rules, with the learning and connectionist structure of neural networks. The main strength of Neuro-Fuzzy systems [7] is that they are universal approximations with the ability to solicit interpretable IF-THEN rules.

2 Available Transfer Capability

ATC [1] is a measure of the transfer capability remaining in the physical transmission network for further commercial activity over and above already committed uses. Mathematically, ATC is defined as the Total Transfer Capability (TTC) less the Transmission Reliability Margin (TRM), less the Capacity Benefit Margin (CBM). ATC = TTC – TRM – CBM.

3 Adaptive Neuro Fuzzy Inference System (ANFIS)

The proposed on-line monitoring [10] of ATC at load dispatch center using ANFIS is shown in Fig.1.The inputs and output of trained ANFIS are voltage magnitudes, phase angles, convergence status, real power and ATC respectively.

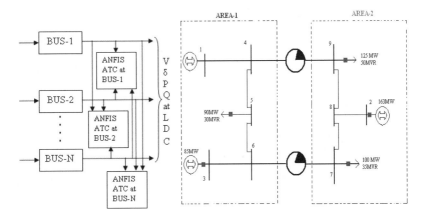

Fig. 1. Proposed ATC using ANFIS   **Fig. 2. IEEE** 9-bus simulation test case

4   Test System and Simulation Results

In this paper, the IEEE 9-bus test system as shown in Fig.2 is considered for analysis and the results are obtained through the following two methods.

4.1   Conventional Method

In this method, the RPF uses the Newton Raphson method in polar coordinates to run the power flow on considered IEEE-9 bus system by enhancing the load in small steps at various buses, with constant power factor, till the method is not converged.

Case 1: *Varying the load at bus-9 without contingency*
    The load is enhanced from the base case in small steps at Bus-9, to enhance the power transfer from area-1 to area-2, till the method (RPF) is not converged and the corresponding results are shown in table-1.

Case2: *Varying the load at bus-9 with contingency*
    In this case to consider the contingency, the branch between Bus-6 and Bus-7 is shut-off, so that the power transferred from the area-1 to area-2 is only through Bus-4 and Bus-9. Similar to the case-1 the load is enhanced at Bus-9 and the corresponding results are shown in table-2.

Table 1. Varying the load at bus-9 without contingency

Load at bus 9(S_9) (MVA)	Converged YES/NO	TTC (MW)	Conventional ATC (MW)
125+j50	YES	225	0
185+j74	YES	285	60
225+j90	YES	325	100
305+j122	YES	405	180
379.8+j151.12	YES	479.8	254.8
379.9+j151.96	NO	479.9	254.9

Table 2. Varying the load at bus- 9 with contingency

Load at bus 9(S_9) (MVA)	Converged YES/NO	TTC (MW)	Conventional ATC (MW)
135+j54	YES	235	10
195+j78	YES	295	70
255+j102	YES	355	130
315+j126	YES	415	190
350.8+j140.32	YES	450.8	225.8
350.9+J140.36	NO	450.9	225.9

4.2   ANFIS Method

The load flow data obtained from the conventional method is given as targets and inputs to train the ANFIS and its performance is checked with the checking data of same conventional method. The proposed ATC values are obtained from the trained ANFIS by giving the new set of power values. The results are compared using graphs as shown in Fig. 3 & 4.

Case 3: *Varying the load at bus-9 without contingency*
    Similar to the case-1 the proposed ATC values are obtained from the trained ANFIS and are compared with the conventional method as shown in table-3.

Case 4: *Varying the load at bus-9 with contingency*

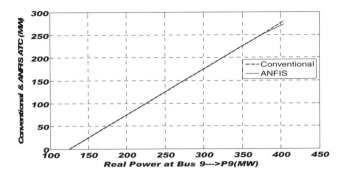

Fig. 3. P-ATC plot for variation of load at Bus-9 without contingency

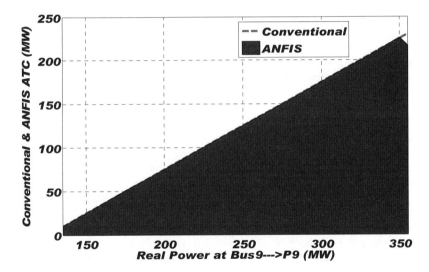

Fig. 4. P-ATC area plot for variation of load at Bus-9 with contingency

Table 3. Varying the load at bus 9 without contingency

Test Pattern	Load at bus 9(S₉) (MVA)	Converged YES/NO	Conventional ATC (MW)	ANFIS ATC (MW)	% Error
1	125+j50	YES	0	0	0
2	145+j58	YES	20	19.8	1
3	185+j74	YES	60	60.1	-0.16
4	225+j90	YES	100	99.7	0.3
5	265+j106	YES	140	140.4	-0.285
6	305+j122	YES	180	179.6	0.222
7	345+j138	YES	220	220.8	-0.36
8	379+j151.6	YES	254	252.6	0.55
9	405+j162	NO	280	273.3	2.39
Under operating conditions the accuracy of ANFIS ATC as compared to conventional ATC is 99.64%					

Table 4. Varying the load at bus 9 with contingency

Test Pattern	Load at bus 9(S_9) (MVA)	Converged YES/NO	Conventional ATC (MW)	ANFIS ATC (MW)	% Error
1	135+j54	YES	10	9.9	1
2	155+j62	YES	30	30	0
3	175+j70	YES	50	50.1	-0.2
4	195+j78	YES	70	70	0
5	215+j86	YES	90	90	0
6	255+j102	YES	130	130	0
7	295+j118	YES	170	169.9	0.058
8	315+j126	YES	190	190	0
9	335+j134	YES	210	209.9	0.0476
10	350+j140	YES	225	225.8	-0.355
11	355+j142	NO	230	216.9	5.69
Under operating conditions the accuracy of ANFIS ATC as compared to conventional ATC is 99.86%					

Similar to the case-2 the proposed ATC values are obtained from the trained ANFIS and are compared with the conventional method, shown in table-4.

5   Conclusion

When the system is in operation, the overall accuracy of ANFIS ATC as compared to the conventional ATC with and without contingency is 99.86% and 99.64% respectively. Therefore the percentage of error may be overcome by training the ANFIS in an on-line. The quantity of ATC increases with the increase of load. Modeling of the system using conventional methods based on mathematical equations is limited by several constraints, involves complex calculations and iterative in nature so these methods may not give the desired solutions when implementing in an on-line. The only alternative to model the system is by considering the existing data of system using hybrid intelligent techniques. The proposed ANFIS ATC does not involve any iterations or complex calculations, so it takes less time to compute and the results shows accurate. Hence the proposed method is the best to monitor the ATC in an on-line at load dispatch centers under the deregulated environment.

References

1. Gopi Krishna, P., Gowri Manohar, T.: Voltage stability constrained ATC computations in Deregulated Power System using novel technique. ARPN Journal of Engineering and Applied Sciences 3(6) (December 2008) ISSN 1819-6608
2. Kamaraj, N., Venkatesan, S.: Dynamic rescheduling model for congestion management with real power transaction. In: International, Power Engineering Conference, IPEC 2007, pp. 741–746 (2007)
3. Available Transfer Capability Definitions and Determination (1996), http://www.nerc.com

4. Ilic, M.D., Yoon, Y.T., Zobian, A.: Available transfer capacity (ATC) and its value under open access. IEEE Trans. Power Syst. 12, 636–645 (1997)
5. Jang, J.-S.R.: ANFIS: Adaptive-Network-based Fuzzy Inference Systems. IEEE Transactions on Systems, Man, and Cybernetics 23(3), 665–685 (1993)
6. Kumar, A., Srivastava, S.C.: Available transfer capability assessment in a competitive electricity market using a bifurcation approach. Generation Transmission and Distribution, IEE Proceedings 151(2), 133–140 (2004)
7. Limpatthamapanee, S., Phichaisawat, S.: Determination of transfer capability using ANFIS with system condition separability. Electrical Engineering/ Electronics Computer, Telecommunications and Information Technology 01 (2009), doi: 10.1109 /ECTICON
8. Nakawiro, W., Erlich, I.: Online Voltage Stability Monitoring using Artificial Neural Network. In: DRPT 2008, Nanjing, China, April 6-9 (2008)
9. Luo, X., Patton, A.D., Singh, C.: Real power transfer capability calculations using multi-layer feed-forward neural networks. IEEE Trans. Power Syst. 15 (February 2000)
10. Ramesh, R., Ramachandran, V.: Online Monitoring of Multi-Area Power Systems in Distributed Environment. Serbian Journal of Elec. Engg. 3 (June 2006)
11. Nguyen, T.T.: Neural network load-flow. Generation, Transmission and Distribution, IEE Proceedings 142(1), 51–58 (1995)
12. de Souza, A.C.Z., de Souza, J.C.S., da Silva, A.M.L.: On-line voltage stability monitoring. IEEE Transactions on Power Systems 15(4) (November 2000)
13. Phadke, A.R., Fozdar, M., Niazi, K.R.: A New Technique for on-line Monitoring of Voltage Stability Margin Using Local Signals. In: 15th NPSC IIT, Bombay (December 2008)

A Novel Technique for Indication of Power Frequency Deviations in Electrical Systems

Jitendra Dwivedi[1,*], M. Shukla[1,*], K.S. Verma[2], and R.K. Singh[3]

[1] Harcourt Butler Technological Institute, Kanpur, India
jkdagra@indiatimes.com
[2] Kamla Nehru Institute of Technology, Sultanpur, India
ksv02@rediffmail.com
[3] Kumaun Engineering College, Dwarhat, India

Abstract. In this paper, a method for measuring the power frequency deviations has been presented. This technique is based on concept of counting the known train of pulses for the period corresponding to power frequency deviation. It has been simulated on SIMULINK tool of MATLAB and has been duly implemented. The technique is insensitive to harmonic noise due to its ability to filter out all the higher order components. With modest averaging, the approach is also relatively insensitive to offsets and random noise. The simulation results demonstrate a linear relationship between frequency deviation and counted pulses.

Keywords: Frequency deviation, filter, train of pulses, logical operations.

1 Introduction

The power line frequency deviations are prime reasons of concerns for power quality. An accurate estimate of frequency is mandatory for measurements of power and energy signals, especially when a small observation window is required. It is always desired to maintain the frequency of a power system close to its nominal value in each possible case. The accurate measurement of frequency deviation is important in terms of lot of applications such as design of power system stabilizers, power system monitors, communication systems, etc. A number of circuits, which can accurately measure the frequency deviation, are proposed in the literature by researchers [1-4]. However, the circuit discussed are quite complex. Here, we present a very simple strategy for measurement of power frequency deviation which will effectively safeguard the electrical systems.

Section 2 contains an introduction of the techniques used for low frequency deviation measurement in the literature. In section 3, we have introduction to MANJA technique for measurement of power frequency deviation measurement. In section 4, we present the MATLAB implementation of MANJA technique using SIMULINK tool. Section 5 presents computer simulation results of MANJA technique. Section 6 concludes the paper.

---

[*] Authors are with Electrical/ Electronics Engineering Departments

V. V Das, J. Stephen, and N. Thankachan et al. (Eds.): PEIE 2010, CCIS 102, pp. 80–82, 2010.
© Springer-Verlag Berlin Heidelberg 2010

2 Various Frequency Deviation Measurement Techniques

The first method considered in [1], is based on the multiplication of two incoming frequencies by a large factor. A BCD up/down counter is used to count train of pulses in the up mode and another train of pulses in the down mode. In another approach [2], the input signal, for which the frequency deviation measurement is required, is passed through a zero-crossing detector to convert it into a pulse train A. The same input signal is applied to a phase shifting circuit of 90 degrees. The phase-shifted signal, B, is then converted into other pulse train. A two arm bridge is then used to obtain the frequency difference.

In [3], a binary-coded decimal up/down counter is used to find the difference in pulse count, which is indication of frequency deviation. All the discussed techniques are quite inaccurate and slow.

3 Implementation Methodology

This paper describes a relatively simple method for measuring accurately and displaying the line frequency deviation from its nominal value. Increasing the frequency of the pulse generator may increase the accuracy of the method.

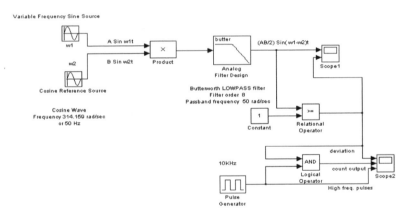

Fig. 1. SIMULINK Model of MANJA Technique

Let $A \sin \omega 1t$ is the input frequency signal for which the deviation is to be measured. Another frequency signal, which is generally taken as cosine function of reference frequency, is, $B \cos \omega_2 t$. These two signals are mixed in multiplier block. The output of the multiplier block is $(AB/2)\left[Sin(\omega_1 - \omega_2)t + Sin(\omega_1 + \omega_2)t\right]$. When, the output of the multiplier is fed to the Sallen-Key filter, the component $(AB/2)\left[Sin(\omega_1 + \omega_2)t\right]$ is filtered out while $(AB/2)\left[Sin(\omega_1 - \omega_2)t\right]$ is allowed. The later component is used to pass the known train of pulses for counting equivalent to frequency deviation from standard value.

4 Simulation Results

The system is tested using sinusoidal input in the frequency range from 45 Hz to 55 Hz with steps of 0.5 Hz in SIMULINK of MATLAB software. Table 1 shows the cases when the frequency of pulse train is set to be 100 KHz respectively.

Table 1. For sampling frequency =10000 Hz and referemce frequency=*50Hz*

Frequency (in Hz)	Frequency Deviation (in Hz)	No. of pulses for ON time
45.0	5.0	10000
45.5	4.5	11111
46.0	4.0	12500
46.5	3.5	14286
47.0	3.0	16667
47.5	2.5	20000
48.0	2.0	25000
48.5	1.5.	33334
49.0	1.0	50000
49.5	0.5	100000
50.0	00	
50.5	0.5	100000

As expected, we can conclude as we increase the frequency of the pulse train, the accuracy of the measurement is increased as well.

5 Conclusion

A novel technique has been proposed for measuring the disturbances in power frequency which is an important factor in power quality. The proposed technique may be used either with a fixed or variable sampling frequency. The technique is not sensitive to harmonic noise because of its ability to filter out all the higher order components. With modest averaging the approach is also relatively insensitive to offsets and random noise with lowest computational complexity.

References

1. Kasparis, T., Voulgaris, N.C., Halkias, C.C.: A method for the precise measurement of the difference between two low frequencies. IEEE Trans. Instrumentation and measurement 34(1) (1985)
2. Ahmad, M.: Power System Frequency Deviation Measurement Using an Electronic Bridge. IEEE Trans. Instrumentation and measurement 37(1) (1985)
3. Voulgaris, N.C., Hamilakis, V.: An accurate method for the Measurement of line frequency and its deviation using Microprocessor. IEEE Trans. Instrumentation and measurement 36(1) (1987)

Novel Auxiliary Switch Very-High-Frequency Zero Current Switching Resonant DC-DC Boost Converter

K. Thiruppathi[1], S. Vinodha[2], and R. Kirubagaran[3]

[1] Project Scientist, NIOT (National Institute of Ocean Technology) Govt. of India,
Chennai, India
thiru@niot.res.in
[2] Lecturer, EEE, Jerusalem college of Engineering, Chennai
Svino_eee@yahoo.co.in
[3] Scientist – F, MB-Group head, NIOT (National Institute of Ocean Technology),
kiruba@niot.res.in

Abstract. This paper explores the design of Novel Auxiliary switch dc-dc boost power converter operating in the Very High Frequency range**.** The main switch and auxiliary switch operate at zero-current-switching (ZCS) turn on and turn off. Besides operating at constant frequency and reducing commutation losses, this new converter have no additional current stress and conduction loss in the main switch in comparison to the hard switching converter counterpart. These methods are applied to the development of a 26W resonant boost converter operating at a switching frequency of 30MHz. Design of power stage, hardware design procedure, simulation result and hardware results are treated in detail. For demonstration, a prototype Novel Auxiliary switch system is designed and implemented with discrete components to deliver 26W peak power with 88.9% of efficiency.

Keywords: Multiresonant converter, resonant converter, resonant gating, zero-current-switching, zero-voltage-switching.

1 Introduction

The Zero Current Switching (ZCS) resonant technique is praised for its high power capability, fast transient response and ease of control. The Resonant dc-dc converters have also been widely used in industry. For minimization of size and weight, increasing switching frequency in the resonant converter is required. However, increasing switching frequency will result in the more switching losses and electromagnetic interference (EMI). Recently ,for improving this problem, a number of soft-switching technique were proposed aimed at combining desirable features of both the Very High Frequency and resonant techniques [1]-[4]. The switching losses and the high frequency of operation are two well-known problems [2].In order to overcome previous problems, a number of ZCS Resonant techniques have been proposed [4]. In the Approaches proposed in [2] and [6], ZCS of the active switches is achieved by using a resonant inductor in series with the main switch and a resonant

V. V Das, J. Stephen, and N. Thankachan et al. (Eds.): PEIE 2010, CCIS 102, pp. 83 – 86, 2010.
© Springer-Verlag Berlin Heidelberg 2010

capacitor in series which leads to a substantial increase in conduction loss. This
phenomenon is eliminated in the approaches proposed in [8] by the resonating current
for ZCS flows only through the auxiliary circuit, thus, the current stress of the main
switch is eliminated. But it presents two power diodes in the power transfer path,
which increases conduction losses of the diodes [3].This paper proposes a new ZCS
Resonant auxiliary circuit that improves the drawbacks of the previously proposed
ZCS Resonant converters. The proposed auxiliary circuit provides ZCS condition for
both the main switches and auxiliary Switch the conduction loss and current stress of
the main switch are minimized. A new family of DC-DC converters based on the
proposed ZCS Resonant switch cell is proposed. Besides operating at constant
frequency and with reduced commutation losses, these new converters have no
additional current stress and conduction losses in the main switch in comparison to
the hard switching converter counterpart.

2   The Novel Auxiliary Circuit for Resonant Boost Topology

Fig.1 shows a schematic and ideal characteristic wave form of the new Novel auxiliary
switch resonant dc–dc boost converter topology. This paper presents a converter operating with soft commutation at the main switches and the auxiliary switch devices. The
design is optimized for low device current stress and Very High Frequency (VHF) operation at a fixed frequency and duty ratio. This enables the use of resonant gating and
zero-current switching for high efficiency. The converter can be viewed as a special
version of resonant boost converter because it has one auxiliary switch in addition with
main switch. To improve the accuracy of the model as regards circuit dynamics and
loss, several additional aspects of the power circuit components are considered in the
converter design proceeds by first creating a model for a simulation program such as
SPICE. Then after simulation result analysis some modifications are done based on
results in the power circuit component value after that Hardware circuit model was
designed.

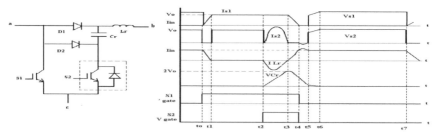

Fig. 1. Proposed new novel auxiliary circuit and ideal characteristic curve for the proposed circuit

3   Design Procedures and Simulation Result

The switches of the minority carrier type devices such as IGBT's are used as main
switch and auxiliary switch, since their commutations are ZCS. A special care should

be taken to design the resonant inductor (Lr) and resonant capacitor (Cr). When the resonance between resonant Inductor and capacitor happens, at resonance the voltage across the capacitor must reach a value twice the input applied voltage and the Inductor current should be Zero.

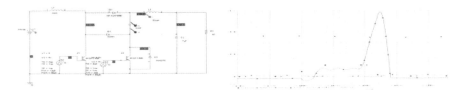

Fig. 2. Simulation circuit and simulated wave form for the proposed circuit

Blue - Resonating capacitor voltage wave form: Red - Resonating Inductor current wave form: Green –Switching pulse: Yellow – Output voltage.

4 Experimental Result and Result Analysis

A 26W, 30-MHz prototype of the proposed Novel auxiliary switch ZCS dc-dc converter has been built and tested to verify the resonance operation. The current through switches are zero before turning off and, it is turned off with complete ZCS, and no tail current is exhibited. The communication phenomenon in the main switch S1, auxiliary switch S2, auxiliary diode D1, and main diode D2, are measured. The experimental results demonstrate that zero-current switching is achieved at constant frequency for both active switches (S1 and S2).Therefore, the switching energy losses for this new ZCS Resonant boost converter are theoretically zero, but practically it is negligible.Fig.3. shows the generated hardware switching pulses for power circuit operation. Finally the entire ideal, simulated and hardware output results are compared and deviations are analyzed.Fig 4 and Fig.5 shows the ideal, simulated and hardware results of the capacitor voltage across the resonant capacitor and Inductor current flowing through resonant inductor respectively.

Table 1. Experimental DC- DC converter specifications

Nominal Input voltage	16V
Nominaloutput voltage	21V
Input voltage range	12– 8V
Output voltage range	15– 5V
Switching frequency	30 MHZ
Nominal output power	26 W
Gatedriveinput voltage	5 V

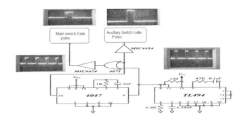

Fig. 3. Hardware output for the proposed design

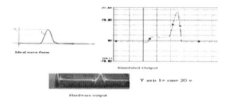

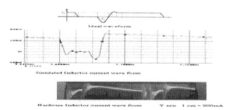

Fig. 4. Ideal, simulated and hardware capacitor voltage

Fig. 5. Ideal, simulated and hardware inductor current

5 Conclusion

This paper has presented a new resonant topology suitable for boost power conversion. The new topology addresses several short comings of previous designs, while maintaining all desirable properties necessary for VHF power conversion, zero-Current switching and absorption of device capacitance. The design implementations described in this paper are expected to contribute to the development of VHF dc–dc converters, paving the way for power electronics that can satisfy the needs for improved size, cost, and performance that are demanded by modern applications.

References

[1] Hua, G., Leu, C.S., Jiang, Y., Lee, F.C.: Novel zero-voltage-transition PWM converter. IEEE Trans. Power Electron. 9(2), 213–219 (1994)

[2] Hua, G., Leu, C.S., Jiang, Y., Lee, F.C.: Novel zero-current-transition PWM converter. IEEE Trans. Power Electron. 9(6), 601–606 (1994); 57(5), 221–226 (1987)

[3] Phinney, J.W., Perreault, D.J., Lang, J.H.: Radio-frequency inverters with transmission-line input networks. IEEE Trans. Power Electron. 22(44), 1154–1161 (2007)

[4] Rivas, J.M., Han, Y., Leitermann, O., Sagneri, A.D., Perreualt, D.J.: A high-frequency resonant inverter topology with low-voltage stress. IEEE Trans. Power Electron. 23(4), 1759–1771 (2008)

Vulnerable Load Bus Identification Using Radial Basis Neural Network

Gauri Shankar[1], Bhavik Suthar[2], R. Balasubramanian[3], and Prince Ashok[3]

[1] Electrical Engineering Department, North Eastern Regional Institute of Science & Technology, Itanagar, Arunachal Pradesh, India
gauri1983@gmail.com
[2] Electrical Engineering Department, Govt. Engineering College, Modasa Gujrat, India
bhavikiitd@yahoo.co.in
[3] Centre for Energy Studies, Indian Institute of Technology, Delhi, India
{balu,princerit}@ieee.org

Abstract. This paper presents a study on effectiveness of artificial neural network in estimating the voltage instability. An ANN model based on radial basis function is designed to predict accurately the voltage collapse phenomenon. In the present study, L-index is used as the voltage collapse proximity indicators. ANN model using radial basis function is trained to identify vulnerable buses in power system which contributes maximally in bringing system to the point of voltage collapse. Modeling is done using a sample 5-bus system and results obtained are quite promising with minimum error in predicting voltage collapse.

Keywords: Voltage stability, Voltage collapse, VCPI, ANN, RBF.

1 Introduction

In recent years, several major voltage collapses have been observed in different parts of the world. Most of the collapses were found due to system being over stressed and non-availability of reactive power sources to maintain normal voltage profile at receiving end buses [1-3]. As a consequence of load increase, there is gradual decrease in bus voltages in the beginning and becomes abrupt after sometimes causing abnormally low voltages in a significant part of the power system [4]. Therefore, voltage stability studies has become an evitable part of power system planning and expansion with main objective to explore the process of evaluation of system conditions, which gradually take the system nearer to the system voltage instability and ultimately to voltage collapse condition.

In order to provide cost-effective, reliable and good quality electrical power supply to consumers power system engineers have been dedicatedly working to develop indicators that would be useful in monitoring the states of the power system. A variety of dynamic and steady-state (static) based approaches have been proposed for the voltage stability studies. Dynamic approach being complex and time consuming, a number of voltage collapse proximity indicators (VCPI) have been developed based on static approaches to readily provide information about how far is our system from the point of voltage collapse [5]. Some of the stability indices developed are based on

V. V Das, J. Stephen, and N. Thankachan et al. (Eds.): PEIE 2010, CCIS 102, pp. 87–90, 2010.
© Springer-Verlag Berlin Heidelberg 2010

minimum singular values of Jacobian matrix, multiple solutions of power flow equations, sensitivity analysis, energy margin and Q-margin [6-12].

Artificial Neural Networks (ANN) has been emerged as the most powerful approach in artificial intelligence (AI) for solving certain traditional problems in power systems where conventional techniques have failed to achieve the desired speed, accuracy or efficiency. ANN has successfully been applied in solving various problems of power systems such as load forecasting, fault diagnosis, load flows and voltage stability [13-16].

In this paper voltage stability studies based on L-index is analyzed on a sample 5 - bus test system [4]. The bus with highest value of the index indicates the most vulnerable bus. The same L-index is used for designing radial basis function (RBF) based ANN model for predicting voltage collapse phenomena.

2 Methodology

Kessel and Glavitch [4] has introduced voltage collapse proximity indicator based on L-index for two bus system then generalized for multi-bus system. Consider a system with n number of buses which includes $1, 2... g$ as generator buses and $g+1, g+2 ... n$ *as load buses.* Load flow program was run for base case and the results obtained were used to calculate L-index as

$$ L_j = \left| 1 - \sum_{i=1}^{g} F_{ji} \frac{V_i}{V_j} \right| \tag{1} $$

Where $j = g+1 ... n$ i.e., $j \in$ set of load buses and $i \in$ set of generator buses and V_i and V_j of the above equation are complex quantities. The values of F_{ji} are obtained from Y-bus matrix and is given by

$$ F^{LG} = -[Y^{LL}]^{-1}[Y^{LG}]. \tag{2} $$

Where $[Y^{LL}]$ and $[Y^{LG}]$ are submatrices of Y-bus matrix.

The bus with the highest value of index is the most vulnerable bus. Thus it is easier to identify in a given power system the weak and healthy part within a system thereby rendering electric power operators to take precautionary measures to avoid voltage collapse. In the present work, real and reactive power loading at load buses and real power generation at generator bus is increased uniformly. It is observed that as the load is increased at the buses, the value of L-index has also increased till the system enters into voltage collapse condition. A number of patterns were generated for different loading conditions and the results obtained were used to train an ANN model based on radial basis function. Because of non-linear nature of RBF, it has exhibited excellent performance in obtaining good approximation modeling complex problems in comparison to multi layer perceptron (MLP) based ANN [17].

3 Application of RBF in Assessing Voltage Stability

A 5-bus system is used for the study which consists of two generator buses, three load buses and six transmission lines [17]. A number of operating conditions is generated by increasing the load factor in step of 0.1 and power factor is kept constant for each case. Simulation was run for each case and necessary training data for neural network is obtained. For each operating conditions, the output of the load flow programs is used to calculate the value of L-index at all the buses. It is observed that as load is increased in step, the value of L-index approached to 1 which is the stability limit of the system.

For training the ANN model based on RBF, a total of 28 sets of input-output vectors have been used corresponding to range of load factors from 1 to 3.05 and the model is validated by 13 sets of randomly generated patterns. Each set of input vectors consists of 10 inputs which include the real and reactive power at the bus 2, 3, 4 and 5 and voltage at bus 1 and 2. And each set of target vectors comprised of voltages at load bus 3, 4 and 5 i.e., V_3, V_4, and V_5 and their corresponding value of L-indices L_3, L_4 and L_5 respectively. It is observed that as the load factor is increased from 1 to 3.05, voltage at all the buses found to be decreasing with corresponding increase in magnitude of L-index. In the given system, the most vulnerable bus is found to be bus 5 with value of L-index being 0.86138 and voltage magnitude going down to 0.5876 corresponding to load factor 3.05. Radial basis network designed is a two layer network with 28 radial basis neurons in the hidden layer. It is observed that ANN model based on radial basis function has correctly predicted the strong and weak operating condition of the power system. Results obtained from ANN as shown in Table: 1 has also ranked bus number 5 as the most vulnerable bus as obtained from the simulation. The L-index for bus 5 obtained from ANN being 0.82049 in comparison to 0.82051 as obtained from simulation corresponding to load factor of 3.035. Mean square error (MSE) observed to be 7.1251e-005, 5.0634e-005 and 4.4079e-005 for L_5, L_4 and L_3 respectively.

Table 1. Comparison between simulation and ANN output

S. No	Load Factor	Results obtained from simulation			Radial basis based ANN results		
		L_3	L_4	L_5	L_3	L_4	L_5
1	1.15	0.04226	0.04283	0.04655	0.0426	0.043195	0.046991
2	1.35	0.05098	0.05161	0.05613	0.0512	0.051798	0.056349
3	1.55	0.06028	0.06095	0.06630	0.0608	0.061500	0.066945
4	1.75	0.07021	0.07091	0.07714	0.0941	0.096554	0.107560
5	1.95	0.15171	0.15753	0.17941	0.1518	0.157630	0.179510
6	2.15	0.18257	0.18984	0.21769	0.1826	0.189840	0.217680
7	2.35	0.21987	0.22900	0.26478	0.2198	0.228900	0.264680
8	2.55	0.26708	0.27873	0.32582	0.2671	0.278710	0.325800
9	2.75	0.33208	0.34756	0.41285	0.3321	0.347520	0.412840
10	2.95	0.44421	0.46742	0.57314	0.4443	0.467490	0.573250
11	3.015	0.52376	0.55347	0.69697	0.5237	0.553440	0.696930
12	3.025	0.54699	0.57879	0.73516	0.5470	0.578800	0.735170
13	3.035	0.59668	0.63326	0.82051	0.5967	0.633240	0.820490

4   Conclusion

The proposed radial basis ANN model based on L-index is quite simple and applied to a 5-bus system. The results obtained were quite promising. The trained network should be useful for the operators for early prediction of voltage collapse. However, it can also be applied successfully applied to large system as well. The proposed ANN model can be used as an alternative tool for on-line voltage stability assessment.

References

1. North American Electric Reliability Council.: Survey of the Voltage Collapse Phenomenon (August 1991)
2. Taylor, C.W.: Power system voltage stability. McGraw-Hill, New York (1994)
3. Kundur, P.: Power System Stability and Control. McGraw- Hill, New York (1994)
4. Kessel, P., Glavitch, H.: Estimating the voltage stability of a power system. IEEE Trans. on power delivery PWRD-1(3), 346–354 (1986)
5. Dobson, I.: The irrelevance of load dynamics for the loading margin to voltage collapse and sensitivities. In: Proc. Bulk Power System Voltage Phenomena III Voltage Stability and Security, pp. 509±18. ECC, Fairfax (August 1994)
6. Tranchit, A., Thomas, R.J.: A Posturing Strategy Against Voltage Instability in Electric Power System. IEEE Trans. on Power Systems, 87–93 (1988)
7. Lof, P.A., Anderson, G., Hill, D.J.: Voltage stability indices for stressed power systems. IEEE Transactions on Power Systems 8, 326–335 (1993)
8. Tamura, Y., Mori, H., Iwamoto, S.: Relationship between Voltage Instability and Multiple Load Flow Solutions in Electric Power Systems. IEEE Trans. on PAS PAS-102(5) (1983)
9. Galiana, F.D., Lee, K.: On the Steady State Stability of Power Systems. In: Proc. of PICA, Toronto (1977)
10. Tamura, Y., Nakanishi, Y., Iwamoto, S.: On the Multiple Solution Structure, Singular Point and Existence Condition of Multiple Load Flow Solutions. In: IEEE/PES Winter Meeting, NY, Paper 043-0 (1980)
11. Gao, B., Morison, G.K., Kundur, P.: Voltage Stability Evaluation Using Modal Analysis. IEEE Transactions on Power System 7(4), 1529–1542 (1992)
12. Lof. P.A., Smed, T., Anderson, G., Hill, D.J.: Fast Calculation of a Voltage Stability Index. Presented at the PES Winter Meeting, New York, paper No. 91 WM 203-0 PWRS (1991)
13. El Sayed, A.H., Alfuhaid, A.S.: ANN-Based Approach for Fast Fault Diagnosis and Alarm Handling of Power System. In: Proc. of 5th International Conference on Advances on Power System Control, Operation and Management, APSCOM 2000, Hong Kong (October 2000)
14. Salama, M.M., Saied, E.M., Abou-Elsaad, M.M., Ghariany, E.F.: Estimating the Voltage Collapse Proximity Indicator using Artificial Neural Network. Energy Conversion & Management 42, 69–79 (2001)
15. Bhavik, S., Balasubramanian, R.: Application of ANN based Voltage Stability Assessment Tool to Restructured Power Systems. In: 2007 iREP Symposium- Bulk Power System Dynamics and Control - VII, Revitalizing Operational Reliability, August 19-24 (2007)
16. Park, J., Sandberg, I.W.: Approximation and Radial Basis Function Networks. Neural Comput. 5, 305–316 (1993)
17. Stagg, G.W., El Abiad Ahmed, H.: Computer Methods in power system analysis. McGraw-Hill, Tokyo (1968)

FPGA Based Design of Robust Spatial Domain Image Watermarking Algorithm

Basu Abhishek[1], Das Tirtha Sankar[2], Nurul Islam[3], and Sarkar Subir Kumar[4]

[1] Abhishek Basu, RCCIIT
idabhishek23@yahoo.com
[2] T S Das, FIEM
tirthasankardas@yahoo.com
[3] N Islam, Narendrapur RKM College[*]
[4]Subir Kumar Sarkar, Jadavpur University
su_sircir@yahoo.co.in

Abstract. The proliferation of digital media creates intimidation towards the security in multimedia data transmission. Watermarking technique becomes a potential solution to this coercion by means of Intellectual Property Right protection, authentication and integrity verification of digital media. As an attempt towards the power efficient system, here we present an oblivious, spatial domain watermarking based authentication algorithm and its FPGA implementation.

Keywords: Embedding system, Image Watermarking, Robust, Spatial Domain, proliferation, Binary Image, FPGA.

1 Introduction

With rapid development of internet and digital consumer devices, access to digital information became vary easier. This leads to the emerging problems like copyright protection, authenticity, integrity verification and security of the digital media. The digital watermarking came as an efficient solution to these problems [1]. Various techniques are introduced and applied to watermarking schemes such as Lower Bit Plane Modulation (Least Significant Bit), Human Visual System (HVS), Spread Spectrum (SS)and Quantization Index Modulation (QIM) [5]. Such schemes when developed in spatial domain provide facility of real time implementation through hardware realization. Software implementations have been developed due to the ease of use, upgrading and flexibility but at the cost of limited speed problem and vulnerability to the offline attack. On the other hand hardware realizations offer advantage over the former in terms of less area, low execution time and low power [6].

The aim of this paper is to develop a spatial image watermarking algorithm that can serve the purpose of digital media authentication as well as secured communication of binary massage signal in real time environment.

Rest of the paper is organized as follows, section II describe the proposed algorithm for watermark embedding and detection. Section III illustrates the hardware

---

[*] Nurul Islam thankfully acknowledges the financial support obtained in the form of U.G.C Minor Research Project.

V. V Das, J. Stephen, and N. Thankachan et al. (Eds.): PEIE 2010, CCIS 102, pp. 91–95, 2010.

realization of proposed method. Section IV represents results and conclusion we made in section V.

2   Watermark Embedding and Detection

The algorithm proposed here is a digital modulation scheme that employs synchronous detection for decoding of the information. The binary image conveys the unique information with a good degree of resiliency after various forms of image impairments. The cover data is considered as a carrier, a gray scale watermarked image called as modulated signal is generated using spatial domain LSB modulation scheme.

In the watermark encoder, the 2-D pixel values of the gray cover as well as binary message are quantized into their stored integer (SI) data type with respective word lengths followed by individual 1-D signal conversion having new frame size redistribution by the buffer block. The binary message string is then redundantly embedded into suitable LSB plane of cover pixels using a pseudorandom (PN) sequence corresponding to a specific state. As the data hiding operation is over, the unbuffer block unbuffers frame-based input into a sample-based output and further converted into 2-D watermarked image.

Similarly, the stego image with or without external attack is transformed to 1-D sequence having SI type pixel values with fixed point quantization in the watermark decoder. The embedded binary data is picked from the bit plane specified by the same private key being used during data embedding and the final estimated bit has been selected using a majority rule. These values represent the pixel values of the decoded message signal. Finally, the same buffer and unbuffer blocks are required here also for the speed of response compatibility.

3   Hardware Realization of Proposed Method

The high density techniques of current FPGAs will be a highly attractive solution for hardware implementation of the watermarking algorithm. The synthesis of the watermark embedding and decoding have been implemented on Xilinx (ISE version 9.2i) based FPGA [9]. Spartan series of FPGA (device: xc3s500e-4ft256) are chosen to fit the complexity of the design. The behavioral simulations were done with Modelsim SE 6.3f and test benches were written in VHDL to give the input vectors for the simulated programs. The design consists of following two parts:

A)   Watermark Embedding

Our design is a generic one so the cover image and watermark image size can be varied. An array of image pixels is taken as input to the encoder in addition to clock, active low reset and array of bit containing watermark. The pixels stored in data buffer which later used to stock up the modified data after watermark embedding. From data buffer one by one image pixels send to comparator which is a combinational circuit determines the perceptually significant pixel values for watermarking. The combinational function is given in (1) for threshold value of 200. After embedding the data sent to the data buffer to store the customized pixel. On the other hand if a pixel less than threshold it directly sent to data buffer.

$$f(A, B, C, D, E, F, G, H) = ABC'DE' + ABCDE' + ABCD'E' + ABEF + ABEF' \quad (1)$$

B) Watermark Decoding

In the input watermarked data taken as array of image pixels with clock and active low reset. The data stored in data buffer thereafter one by one pixels sent to the same combinational circuit called comparator which used in the encoder to compute the threshold limit and to select the perceptually significant, appropriate pixels. Then the hidden watermark bit in the third bit plane is selected and loaded into the massage buffer.

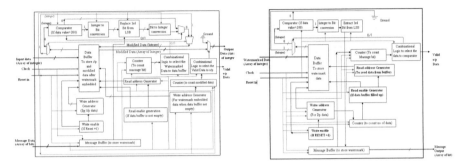

Fig 1. Block Diagram of Watermark Encoder   **Fig 2.** Block Diagram of Watermark decoder

4 Results & Discussion

A) Performance Evaluation

The resiliency performance of the proposed algorithm has been estimated in terms of various image distortions as well as noisy modulated signal similar to the concept of drift in oscillator carrier frequency in synchronous detection. It has been observed that the detected watermarks are quite subjectively recognizable even after a higher depth of degradations occurred in the watermarked image.

Table I. Results For Psnr, Ssim, Security Values And Mutual Information

Image	PSNR(dB)	SSIM	Security value	Mutual Information
Baboon	66.665375	1	0.000070	0.0105784
Pepper	67.597343	1	0.000029	0.0106689
Fishing Boat	67.736435	1	0.000046	0.0105784

B) Results of Hardware Realization

This segment reports the simulation and synthesis results for the proposed design. We consider a 2bits per pixel 2X2 size for massage data and 8bits per pixel 8X8 size for input image for experimental intention. The clock period is taken as 100ns for embedding minimum time required is 6700ns and at 7400ns the process will be complete in case of decoding the output time required is 2300ns. For synthesis purpose we have used Xilinx ISE 9.2i. The top level RTL schematic of the watermark embedding and

Table 2. Design Summary For Embeddingï

Device Utilization Summary [estimated values]			
Logic Utilization	Used	Available	Utilization
Number of Slices	2318	4656	49%
Number of Slice Flip Flops	619	9312	6%
Number of 4 input LUTs	4506	9312	48%
Number of bonded IOBs	135	190	71%
Number of GCLKs	1	24	4%

Table 3. Design Summary For Decoding

Device Utilization Summary [estimated values]			
Logic Utilization	Used	Available	Utilization
Number of Slices	493	4656	10%
Number of Slice Flip Flops	557	9312	5%
Number of 4 input LUTs	816	9312	8%
Number of bonded IOBs	71	190	37%
Number of GCLKs	1	24	4%

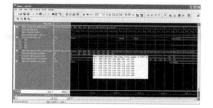

Fig. 3. Behavioral simulation results from Modelsim SE 6.3f for watermark embedding

Fig. 4. Behavioral simulation results from Modelsim SE 6.3f for watermark decoding

Fig. 5. Top level RTL schematic of the embedding system

Fig. 6. Top level RTL schematic of the decoding system

decoding system is given to establish the fact that the HDL codes are synthesizable. For optimization of area we have used a single buffer to store the input data and the embedded data in the embedding section.

5 Conclusion

An algorithm for spatial domain oblivious watermarking and its VLSI realization using FPGA is proposed in this paper. Subjective recognition of the decoded message is possible without the original cover image i.e. the scheme is blind. The algorithm is simple with low computation cost and can be easily implemented in hardware thus suitable for real time authentication as well as secured communication. Current work is going on to develop the dedicated digital system using FPGA chip.

References

[1] Wu, M., Liu, B.: Multimedia Data Hiding. Springer, New York (2002)
[2] Cox, I.J., Miller, M., Bloom, J.: Digital Watermarking. Morgan Kaufmann Publishers, San Francisco (2002)

[3] Cox, I.J., Kilian, J., Leighton, F.T., Shamoon, T.: Secure Spread spectrum watermarking for multimedia. IEEE Transaction on Image Processing 6, 1673–1687 (1997)

[4] Barni, M., Bartolini, F., Piva, A.: Improved Wavelet based Watermarking through Pixel wise Masking. IEEE Trans. on Image Processing 10(5), 783–791 (2001)

[5] Das, T.S., Mankar, V.H., Sarkar, S.K.: Spread Spectrum based Mary Modulated Robust Image Watermarking. IJCSNS International Journal of Computer Science and Network Security 7(10), 154–160 (2007)

[6] Mathai, N.J., Kundur, D., Sheikholeslami, A.: Hardware implementation perspectives of digital video watermarking algorithms. IEEE Transaction on Signal Processing 51, 925–938 (2003)

[7] Image Watermarking Algorithm for a Digital Camera. In: IEEE Conf., pp.1000–1003 (2003)

[8] Mohanty, S.P., Kumar, R.C., Nayak, S.: FPGA based Implementation of an Invisible-Robust Image Watermarking Encoder. In: Das, G., Gulati, V.P. (eds.) CIT 2004. LNCS, vol. 3356, pp. 344–353. Springer, Heidelberg (2004)

[9] Kilmartin, L.: Xilinx FPGA Implementation of an Image Classifier for Object Detection Applications (2007)

A High Performance Direct Torque Control of PMBLDC Motor Using Hybrid (GA Based Fuzzy Logic) Controller

E. Kaliappan[1], C. Sharmeela[2], and A.V. Sayee Krishna[3]

[1] Research scholar, Anna university, Chennai
[2] Senior lecturer, Anna university, Chennai
[3] P.G. student, R.M.K. Engg. College, Chennai

Abstract. This paper deals with the direct torque control of PMBLDC motor using hybrid (Genetic algorithm based fuzzy logic) controller to improve the performance of the control scheme. Though the conventional controllers are commonly used in practice, they have failed to perform satisfactorily under non linear conditions and parameter variations. In the proposed work, a hybrid controller (using genetic algorithm based fuzzy logic controller) is introduced to control the torque and the flux linkage angle of the PMBLDC motor. Torque error and flux linkage angle of the PMBLDC motor is fuzzified and it is auto tuned by GA to improve the dynamic characteristic. Simulation results of the conventional fuzzy logic controller are compared with the hybrid (GA based fuzzy logic) controller and the later is found to be satisfactory with improved performance.

Keywords: PMBLDC motor, Fuzzy logic control, Direct Torque Control (DTC), Genetic algorithm.

1 Introduction

Direct Torque Control is one method used in variable frequency drives to control the torque of a 3 phase motor [1][2] which has some attractive features like fast dynamic response, smooth and fast control of torque and flux angle. Fuzzy logic and Fuzzy set was introduced by Zadeh [3][4]. The application of a FLC in the field of electric drives especially in switched reluctance motor, induction motor and PMBLDC motors have increased in recent times [5]. However the conventional FLC with multiple inputs having multiple membership functions and multiple rules have been facing some disadvantages due to its high computational burden [6]. To overcome the above difficulties GA based FLC has been implemented in the proposed work.

2 Ga Tuned Fuzzy Logic Controller Based DTC

In the proposed work seven triangular fuzzy sets have been used to partition the input and output spaces: negative large (NL), negative medium (NM), negative small (NS), zero (ZE), positive small (PS), positive medium (PM), positive large (PL).the rule set then contains forty nine (7x7) rules to account for every possible combination of the input fuzzy sets. The rules are of the form, IF (x is {NL, NM, NS, ZE, PS, PM, PL})

V. V Das, J. Stephen, and N. Thankachan et al. (Eds.): PEIE 2010, CCIS 102, pp. 96–99, 2010.
© Springer-Verlag Berlin Heidelberg 2010

and (v is {NL, NM, NS, ZE, PS, PM, PL}) THEN {output}, where output is one of the fuzzy sets used to partition the outer space as listed in table I. The basic block diagram of the proposed GA [7] based FLC is shown in Fig. 1. GA parameters in table II consists of a voltage and current measurement block from where the measured Dc bus voltage and current are given to the torque and flux calculator and the abc variables are transformed to dq variables. The optimized values are defuzzified and again transformed to abc variables and the same is given to the switching circuit.

Table 1. Rule Base For DTC Scheme

e(u) ce(u)	NL	NM	NS	ZE	PS	PM	PL
NL	NL	NL	NL	NL	NM	NS	ZE
NM	NL	NL	NL	NM	NS	ZE	PS
NS	NL	NL	NM	NS	ZE	PS	PM
ZE	NL	NM	NS	ZE	PS	PM	PL
PS	NM	NS	ZE	PS	PM	PL	PL
PM	NS	ZE	PS	PM	PL	PL	PL
PL	ZE	PS	PM	PL	PL	PL	PL

Table 2. Parameters Of Genetic Algorithm

GA parameters	Values
Population crossover	0.8
Population mutation	0.03
Generation	20
Maximum iteration	15

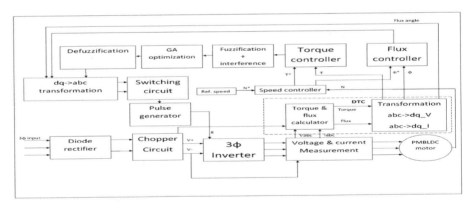

Fig. 1. Basic block diagram of the proposed DTC scheme using GA based FLC

3 Simulation Results

To verify the applicability of the proposed DTC scheme using the hybrid (GA based fuzzy logic) controllers for the PMBLDC motor, simulations were carried out using Matlab. Fig. 2 and 3 shows the performance comparison of the conventional Fuzzy controller and the proposed method using GA based Fuzzy Logic controller for DTC.

Initially DTC scheme using conventional fuzzy logic controller was developed and the performance were compared with the proposed hybrid (GA based fuzzy logic) controller, and the later has an improved performance than the conventional fuzzy logic controller overcoming the drawbacks of the conventional controller.

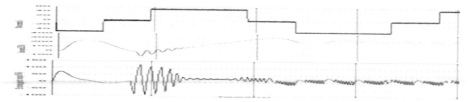

Fig. 2. Simulated performance with conventional Fuzzy logic controller (a) Stator current (b) Rotor speed (c) Electromagnetic torque

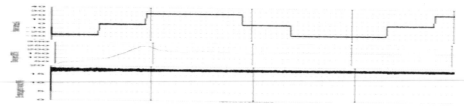

Fig. 3. Simulated performance of the proposed GA based Fuzzy logic controller (a) Stator current (b) Rotor speed (c) Electromagnetic torque

4   Conclusion

In order to prove the superiority of the proposed controller, a performance comparison with conventional FLC has been provided. Simulated results show a better control performance than that of the conventional DTC. The proposed control scheme uses a conventional control rule of DTC, but the switching pulse width is controlled by the torque error. Therefore, a simple implementation but a high control performance can be obtained. The unique feature of this paper is that GA based FLC is very simple with lesser number of membership function and rules.

References

1. Ozturk, S.B., Toliyat, H.A.: Direct torque control of brushless dc motor with non-sinusoidal back-EMF. In: Proc. IEEE-IEMDC Biennial Meeting, Antalya, Turkey, May 3-5 (2007)
2. Zhong, L., Rahman, M.F., Hu, W.Y., Lim, K.W.: Analysis of direct torque control in permanent magnet synchronous motor drives. IEEE Trans. Power Electron. 12(3), 528–536 (1997)
3. Bay, O.F., Elmas, C., Alci, M.: Fuzzy Logic based control of a switched reluctance drive. In: Int. Aegean Conf. Electrical Machines Power Electronics, Kusadasi, Turkey, June 5-7, pp. 333–337 (1995)

4. Elmas, C., Akcayol, M.A.: Fuzzy logic controller based speed control of brushless DC motor. J.Polytechnic 3(3), 7–14 (2000)
5. Mir, S., Eibuluk, M.E., Zinger, D.S.: PI and Fuzzy estimators for tuning the stator resistance in direct torque control of induction machines. IEEE Trans. Power Electron. 13, 179–287 (1998)
6. Lin, C.-L., Jan, H.-Y., Shieh, N.-C.: Genetic algorithm based multiobjective PID control for a linear brushless Dc motor. Transaction on mechatronics of IEEE 8(1), 56–65 (2003)
7. Nasiruddin, M., Abdio, M.A., Rahman, M.A.: Real time performance evaluation of a genetic algorithm based fuzzy logic controller for IPM motor drives. IEEE Trans. on industrial applications 41(1) (January/February 2005)

Embedded System Design and Real Time Hardware Implementation of OLED Interface Card

Himanshu Singh, Sudhir Khare, Ajay Kumar, and S. S. Negi

Thermal Imaging Division,
Instruments Research and Development Establishment, Raipur Road, Dehradun, India

Abstract. The paper discusses about the design and hardware realization of Organic Light Emitting Diode (OLED) interface card with Gap Measuring Device (GMD Mk III) system. The unique feature of this design lies in its being small, lightweight, low power consuming and high brightness/ contrast image. After introduction, the paper elaborates upon the design requirements, hardware design issues, software philosophy through flowchart and finally results and conclusion is given.

Keywords: Organic Light Emitting Diode (OLED), Embedded system, Gap Measuring Device (GMD Mk III).

1 Introduction

The thermal imaging systems division of Instruments' Research and Development Establishment (I.R.D.E.), Dehradun is involved in the development of various classes of Long, Medium and Handheld thermal imagers to meet the user requirements. A thermal imager is an imaging device which can sense the incoming photons and make the visual image of the scene on the display.

A thermal sight for Gap Measuring Device MK-III (GMD MK-III) has been realized which is to be used by Army in field operations for Bridge laying activities. It requires a smaller, portable, lightweight and battery operated system. Therefore, the choice for video display culminated in the selection of Organic Light Emitting Diode (OLED) based display device. It is a miniaturized display based on an emerging and latest display technology. The usefulness of OLED based display is in its being light weight, low power consumption, high brightness and contrast image, wide viewing angle etc. The purpose of this interface card is to:-

a) Establish communication between the microcontroller and the OLED display over I2C (Inter integrated circuit) bus to control its gain and brightness settings;
b) Generation of power supplies (+4V, +3.3V, -3V) from +5V DC necessary for the operation of OLED.

2 Design Requirements

The OLED interface card is mainly designed to interface eMagin Corporation make OLED micro display. The design of card involved the systematic design of power

V. V Das, J. Stephen, and N. Thankachan et al. (Eds.): PEIE 2010, CCIS 102, pp. 100–103, 2010.
© Springer-Verlag Berlin Heidelberg 2010

supply modules, keypad interfacing, microcontroller and its associated electronics module and mounting of OLED.

3 Hardware Design Issues

The OLED display should be initialized during power 'ON' for proper functionality. The microcontroller carries out this operation through I2C bus. It is a 2- wire bus handling data (SDA) and clock (SCL). The microcontroller acts as a Master and initializes the Slave OLED micro display. The OLED display can be configured to operate either in monochrome mode or in colour mode. Upon powering up, the 26 registers of the OLED are initialized with the designated settings programmed into the microcontroller. After initialization, the microcontroller scans the pushbuttons/ signals for user input. If any of the pushbuttons marked for contrast/gain and brightness is pressed by operator and sensed by microcontroller, then it transmits an incremental value to the corresponding register and this affects the contrast and brightness of OLED. The system provides the operator with the option of saving the manually set contrast and brightness values into memory.

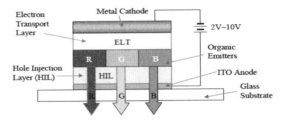

Fig. 1. Organic LED (OLED) operation

3.1 Organic Light Emitting Diode (OLED)

An individual OLED element is a solid-state semiconductor device that is 100 to 500 nanometers thick or about 200 times smaller than a human hair. OLEDs can have either two layers or three layers of organic material. In the latter design, the third layer helps transport electrons from the cathode to the emissive layer. An OLED consists of substrate, anode, organic layer, conducting layer, emissive layer and cathode.

3.2 Microcontroller

The microcontroller used is Silicon Laboratories C8051F007. The C8051F00x family is fully integrated mixed-signal System on a Chip MCUs with a true 12-bit multi-channel ADC. In the design, port 0 is used to receive keypad inputs/ gain and brightness inputs. The internal oscillator is set at a frequency of 8 MHz. The serial communication between microcontroller and the OLED is performed using the I2C bus. This microcontroller was chosen as it has in-built I2C bus configuration.

Setting up of few registers will initialize the I2C bus and communication can be established.

3.3 Power Supply Module

The power supply module is designed to provide power to the following subsystem:-

1. Micro controller module: 3.3 volt (max 12.5 mA)
2. OLED driver module : +4V, +3.3V, -3V

3.4 Keypad Module

A small keypad is interfaced to the card externally to check the operation of the interface card. A key debouncing time of 20 ms is provided through software means. On giving commands, the respective operation is carried out.

4 Software

The software code has been written in the assembly language of C8051F007 microcontroller in the Silicon Laboratories Integrated Development Environment (IDE). The flowchart of the code is given below in fig 2.

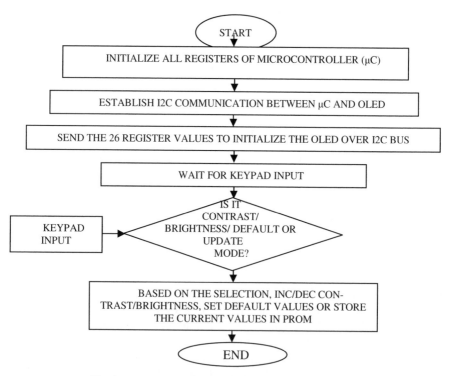

Fig. 2. Flowchart of Software code for OLED Interface Card

5 Results

The results are shown in the form of pictures of the developed system, Hardware pcb and the thermal image on the OLED display. The hardware includes the power supply module and microcontroller interface to the OLED on the same pcb. In fig 3(a), the OLED is shown mounted on the card. In fig 3(b), the thermal image of the scene is shown through the OLED display. In fig. 3(c), the GMD MK III system is shown.

| Fig 3(a) | Fig 3(b) | Fig 3(c) |

6 Conclusions and Future Work

The complete software and hardware of the OLED Interface Card has been developed and interfaced with the Gap Measuring device (GMD Mk III). Presently, the interface card can interface and display the thermal imager video (monochrome) only. But, in future, a color CCD camera with SVGA output will also be interfaced using the same card.

Frequency Detector Using Piezo Laminated Cantilever Beam

B.V.M.P. Santhosh Kumar, U. Varun Kumar, K. Suresh, G. Uma, and M. Umapathy

Department of Instrumentation and Control Engineering,
National Institute of Technology, Tiruchirapalli, India-620015
{umapathy,guma}@nitt.edu

Abstract. A method to measure the frequency of the signal using piezo laminated cantilever beam is proposed. The frequency is detected from the pattern acquired from the sensor output. Electronics for the sensor is built using microcontroller 89C51 and is found to respond over a range of 3-35Hz with a resolution of 1mHz. The sensor is also simulated using COMSOL Multi physics software. The proposed method is simple and it does not consume power from the measurand.

Keywords: Frequency detector; Cantilever beam; Piezoelectric; Micro controller.

1 Introduction

Frequency detection plays a crucial role in modern electrical and electronic systems and is necessary for the purpose of protection and control. These are widely used in signal transmission, where synchronization of frequency is very important. The primary reason for synchronization is to allow generators to be interconnected and operate in parallel. Another important application of the frequency detector is single frequency in-band signaling systems which are widely utilized in telephone equipment to pass address, supervisory and alerting signals for telephone trunks, where a single tone detection circuit is required at each end of the system to detect normal standard signaling tone in the presence of voice and other signals [1]. Number of electronic frequency detectors exists in market today but they struggle in selecting narrow band signals and it is difficult to maintain the accuracy of the centre frequency within the tolerance as mentioned in [1-4]. Moreover they use electronic components which consume power from the measurand. Use of mechanical resonators for detection of frequency is cited in [5-7]. This paper proposes a Piezo laminated cantilever based frequency detector. This has high reliability and does not consume power from the measurand.

2 Measurement System

The measurement system consists of a flexible aluminum beam with fixed clamped end. Two Piezo ceramic patches are surface bonded at a distance of 10 mm from the fixed end

V. V Das, J. Stephen, and N. Thankachan et al. (Eds.): PEIE 2010, CCIS 102, pp. 104–107, 2010.
© Springer-Verlag Berlin Heidelberg 2010

as shown in Fig 1. The Piezo ceramic patch bonded on the bottom surface acts as a sensor and the one on the top surface acts as an actuator or vice versa. A cylindrical permanent magnet of 6.5mm x 2mm with 0.5 Tesla is mounted on the bottom surface of the cantilever beam and an electromagnetic coil of 2000 turns is placed under the magnet.

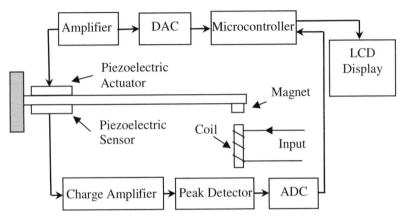

Fig. 1. Piezo actuated cantilever beam frequency Detector

The dimensions and properties of the beam and Piezo ceramic patches are given in Table 1. Considering the sensitivity and the tip displacement of the cantilever beam at resonance, the distance between the coil and the magnet is optimized to be 5×10^{-3} m.

Table 1. Properties and Dimensions of the Aluminum Beam and Piezoelectric patch

Parameters	Aluminum Beam	Piezoelectric Crystal
Length (m)	0.2	0.0765
Width (m)	0.013	0.013
Thickness (m)	0.00127	0.0005
Young's modulus (GPa)	71	47.62
Density (Kg/m^3)	2700	7500
Piezoelectric strain constant (mV^{-1})	NA	-247×10^{-12}
Piezoelectric stress constant (VmN^{-1})	NA	-9×10^{-3}

3   Measurement of Frequency

The signal whose frequency is to be measured is passed through the coil and an excitation signal is applied to the Piezo actuator. When frequency of the excitation signal is swept linearly, the Piezo sensor output is found to be a modulated until the frequencies match and when the frequencies match the sensor output is found to be an unmodulated signal which is a measure of the signal frequency. The results in Fig. 2 show the signal patterns when the frequencies match and when they do not match.

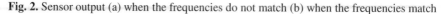

Fig. 2. Sensor output (a) when the frequencies do not match (b) when the frequencies match

3.1 The Experiment

A microcontroller AT 89C51 is programmed to generate a reference signal from LUT (Look up Table) that has 168 data points for single cycle of sinusoidal signal. A DAC 0800 (Digital to Analog Converter) is used to convert this signal into analog form and is directly given as actuating input to the Piezo crystal after amplification. For each input signal, the Piezo sensor output is conditioned and fed back to the microcontroller through ADC 0804 (Analog to Digital Converter). The output of the peak detector is an envelope of the modulated signal, when both the frequencies match the output is a DC signal. Hence, the Microcontroller is programmed to sweep the frequency of the excitation signal from 1Hz to 40Hz by varying the delay between the successive fetches from LUT until a DC signal is obtained at the peak detector. It is further programmed to display the detected frequency on the LCD. The resolution of the structure used in this work is found to be 1mHz for the input range of 3Hz to 35Hz. The experimental results illustrate that the frequencies other than the natural frequency can also be detected.

3.2 Simulation

The sensor is simulated in COMSOL Multi physics 3.5a version software in particular, MEMS structural mechanics module. The structure is built with the dimensions

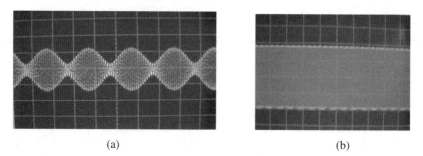

Fig. 3. Displacement amplitude in y-direction (a) when the frequencies match (b) when the frequencies do not match

specified in Table1 and a force analogous to the voltage applied to the Piezo and the voltage applied to the electromagnet is applied on the structure at their respective positions. The simulation is carried out by applying the force with a frequency of 30Hz at both the positions and also by keeping the force constant at one position (30Hz) and sweeping force applied at other position linearly from 0-100Hz. The results are shown in Fig 3.

4 Conclusions

Frequency detector using Piezo laminated cantilever is designed and tested using microcontroller based electronics. It is found to give satisfactory results over a range of 3-35Hz with a resolution of 1mHz. The structure is also simulated in COMSOL Multi physics. The advantage of the proposed system is it does not consume power from the measurand and it can be easily modified to measure frequency over different ranges by altering the dimensions of the structure. The sensor is believed to give better results in micro scale and further work is being carried out to prove the same.

References

1. Miller-Thomson, J.J., Dupuis, G.: Single Frequency Detection Circuit. US patent No: 4546490 (1985)
2. Cheng, T.-Y., Hsinchu.: Analog Phase Frequency Detecting Apparatus and Method. US Patent No: 6501259 (2002)
3. Nguyen, C.T.-C.: Radios with Micromachined Resonators. IEEE Spectrum magazine (December 2009)
4. Kratyuk, V., Hanumolu, P.K., Moon, U.K., Mayaram, K.: Frequency detector for fast frequency lock of digital PLLs. Electronics Letters 43, 13–14 (2007)
5. Smith, L.S., Schenectady, N.Y., Brisken, A. F., Springs, S.: Ultrasonic Transducer for Single Frequency Applications. US patent No: 4366406 (1982)
6. Podgornyi, Y.V.: Frequency Detectors Based on Quartz Resonators in Analytical Devices. Measurement Techniques 47(7), 697–705 (2004)
7. Suna, B., Henry Huang, X.M.: Mechanical nano-resonators at ultra-high frequency and their potential applications. South African Journal of Science 104(5-6), 169–171 (2008)

IMC Based PID Controller Tuning for Unstable SOPDT Processes

V.K. Singh, P.K. Padhy, and S.K. Jain

PDPM Indian Institute of Information Technology, Design & Manufacturing
482005 Jabalpur, India
vinaysi@iiitdmj.ac.in

Abstract. In this paper, PID tuning formulas are derived for unstable second order plus dead time (SOPDT) processes based on IMC principle. To achieve smooth output response, even in the presence of measurement noise, a first order low pass filter is inserted in the process output. Second order low pass filter used in this design reduces the effect of process-model mismatch and thus improves the performance. Examples from previous works are included for comparison, and results confirm the improvement in the disturbance rejection.

Keywords: IMC, Measurement noise, Unstable SOPDT.

1 Introduction

It is a matter of fact that the internal model control (IMC) structure has long been successfully used for controlling open-loop stable plants. However, for unstable processes the IMC structure cannot be implemented directly, reason being internal instability. Also the process output becomes noisy due to the random variation of output signal during the measurement. A lot of academic research had been devoted to developing effective control strategies for unstable processes.

Lee et al. [1] designed an IMC based PID controller for unstable process and integrating process. A set point filter is used in their method to reduce the overshoot which increases the number of design parameter. Huang and Lin. [2] developed a PID tuning for unstable process using optimization technique. The PID parameters are obtained based on the IAE criterion and least-squares method. Jung et al. [3] suggested using a first order set point filter to construct a two-degree-of-freedom control structure for unstable processes. A newly designed method for a disturbance estimator has been proposed for enhanced disturbance rejection in the 2DOF control scheme developed by Liu et al. [5]. However, the methods discussed above have not considered the measurement noise. Filtering is the most convenient possibility to remove the measurement noise. The noise usually occurs at high frequency, while the interest of control design is at low frequency. Therefore, a low pass filter can be used to remove the measurement noise. This paper proposes a modified IMC structure for SOPDT unstable processes with time delays, which enhance set-point disturbance rejection and also reduce the effect of measurement noise in process output. Simple PID tuning formula derived in form series lead-lag filter. Stability conditions are discussed for

V. V Das, J. Stephen, and N. Thankachan et al. (Eds.): PEIE 2010, CCIS 102, pp. 108–112, 2010.

modified IMC structure. Also a smooth output is obtained by using a first order low pass filter in process output.

2 Modified IMC Structure

This paper proposed modified IMC structure (Fig.1.) if only the following conditions are satisfied for the internal stability of the closed-loop system:

(1) G_{IMC} stable.
(2) $G_{IMC}G_P$ stable.
(3) $(1 - G_{IMC} G_P) G_P$ stable.

where process model G_m is divided in two part invertible or delay free part and non invertible or delay part $G_m(s) = G_I(s)*G_{NI}(s)$. Now modified model P(s) can be obtained where (Fig 1).

$$P_I = G_I * \frac{1}{(\beta s + 1)} \qquad\qquad P_{NI} = G_{NI} \qquad (1)$$

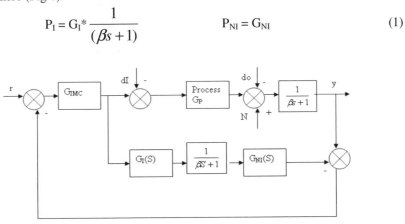

Fig. 1. Modified IMC structure

3 IMC Controller Design

Let the transfer function of the process model be

$$G_m(s) = \frac{Kpe^{-\theta s}}{(T1s-1)(T2s-1)} \qquad (2)$$

The invertible and non-invertible component of modified model P(s)

$$P_I(s) = \frac{Kp}{(\beta s+1)[(T1s-1)(T2s-1)]} \qquad P_{NI}(s) = G_{NI} = e^{-\theta s} \qquad (3)$$

Second step is to define controller as

$$G_{IMC}(s) = P_I^{-1}(s)*f(s) = \frac{(T1s-1)(T2s-1)(\alpha 2s^2+\alpha 1s+1)(\beta s+1)}{Kp(\lambda s+1)^4} \qquad (4)$$

Where $f(s) = \dfrac{\alpha 2 s^2 + \alpha 1 s + 1}{(\lambda s + 1)^4}$ is the low pass filter with adjustable time constant λ

That reduces the effect of process-model mismatch and improves the closed loop performance. The first condition is satisfied because we inversed the process model delay free part now unstable poles become zeros of controller. The RHP poles of G_P must be canceled by the zeros of G_{IMC} eqn. (4) [condition (2)]. The RHP poles of G_P must be canceled by the zeros of $(1 - G_{IMC} *G_P)$ [condition (3)].

$$(1 - G_P G_{IMC}) \,|_{s \to 1/T1,\ 1/T2} = 0 \tag{5}$$

Where $\alpha 1$ and $\alpha 2$ values are calculated with the help of this equation (5).

$$[1 - \dfrac{(\alpha 2 s^2 + \alpha 1 s + 1)(\beta s + 1)e^{-\theta s}}{(\lambda s + 1)^4}\ ]_{s \to 1/T1,\ 1/T2} = 0 \tag{6}$$

The values of α1 and α2 are obtained after simplification and given below

$$\alpha 1 = -(T1+T2)+[\dfrac{(\dfrac{\lambda}{T1}+1)^4 e^{\frac{\theta}{T1}}}{T2^2(\dfrac{\beta}{T1}+1)} - \dfrac{(\dfrac{\lambda}{T2}+1)^4 e^{\frac{\theta}{T2}}}{T1^2(\dfrac{\beta}{T2}+1)}]/[\dfrac{1}{T1T2}(\dfrac{1}{T2}-\dfrac{1}{T1})] \tag{7}$$

$$\alpha 2 = \dfrac{T1^2(\dfrac{\lambda}{T1}+1)^4 e^{\frac{\theta}{T1}}}{T2^2(\dfrac{\beta}{T1}+1)} - (\alpha 1 T1 + T1^2) \tag{8}$$

4   PID Controller Design

The two unstable poles impose a phase lead and time delay terms impose a phase lag. In the present work, to make the controller realizable, a PID controller in series with a lead lag compensator is considered [6]-[7]. IMC controller transform into PID lead-lag filter controller. The dead time $e^{-\theta s}$ is approximated by pade expansion

$$C_{PID}(s) = \dfrac{GIMC}{1 - GIMC * PI * PNI} \tag{9}$$

$$C_{PID}(s) = K_C (1+T_d\, s+1/T_1 *s)\dfrac{(1+as)}{(1+0.1as)} \tag{10}$$

$$CPID = \dfrac{(T1s-1)(T2s-1)(\alpha 2 s^2 + \alpha 1 s + 1)(\beta s+1)(1+\dfrac{\theta}{2}s)}{K_P(\theta+4\lambda-\alpha 1)s[1+\dfrac{(\dfrac{\alpha 1\theta}{2}-\alpha 2+2\lambda\theta+6\lambda^2)}{(\theta+4\lambda-\alpha 1)}s+\dfrac{(\dfrac{\alpha 2\theta}{2}+3\lambda^2\theta+4\lambda^3)}{(\theta+4\lambda-\alpha 1)}s^2+\dfrac{(2\lambda^3\theta+\lambda^4)}{(\theta+4\lambda-\alpha 1)}s^3+\dfrac{(\dfrac{\lambda^4\theta}{2})}{(\theta+4\lambda-\alpha 1)}s^4]} \tag{11}$$

Comparing (10) and (11)

$$K_C = \frac{\alpha 1}{Kp(\theta + 4\lambda - \alpha 1)}; \quad T_I = \alpha 1; \quad Td = \frac{\alpha 2}{\alpha 1}; \quad a = (\beta + \theta/2) \qquad (12)$$

5   Simulation Verification

One example is presented in this section to illustrate the methodology discussed in the preceding section. Also, the method proposed by Liu et al, Lee et al has been considered here for comparison study. Consider the process given in [1] G_P $= \frac{2e^{-0.3s}}{(3s-1)(s-1)}$. The proposed PID with series lead-lag filter gives K_C= 3.224328, T_I = 1.471771, T_d = 1.22656, a = 0.1983, β = 0.0483. Fig 2 shows the unit step output response for λ=0.35 with unit step load at t=20 and random noise N $(0, \sigma^2 = 0.2 * 10^{-4})$ (having SNR=20dB). Overshoot problem can be solved by set-point filter and value of low pass filter constant β can be obtain with the help of [8].

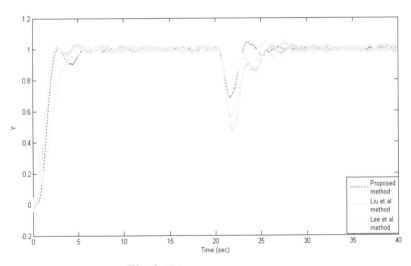

Fig. 2. Unit step output responses

6   Conclusions

A modified IMC structure has been proposed for SOPDT unstable process. The method ensures a de-noised process output even in the presence of measurement noise. A PID controller with series lead-lag filter designed in terms of process model parameter and low pass filter time constant β and closed loop time constant λ from the IMC structure. The controllers perform well for set-point disturbance rejection. The simulation result show that the proposed method gives improved result as compared to some previous work on PID control.

References

1. Lee, Y., Lee, J., Park, S.: PID controller tuning for integrating and unstable processes with time delay. Chem. Eng. Sci. 55, 3481–3493 (2000)
2. Hunang, C.T., Lin, Y.S.: Tuning of PID controller for open loop unstable process with time delay. Chem. Eng. Comm. 133, 11 (1995)
3. Jung, C.S., Song, H.K., Hyun, J.C.: A direct synthesis tuning method of unstable first-order-plus-time-delay processes. Process Control 9, 265–269 (1999)
4. Tan, W., Marquez, H.J., Chen, T.: IMC design for unstable processes with time delay. J. Process Control 13, 203–213 (2003)
5. Liu, T., Zhang, W., Gu, D.: Analytical design of two-degree-of-freedom control scheme for open-loop unstable process with time delay. J. Process Control 15, 559–572 (2005)
6. Shamsuzzoha, M., Moonyong, L.: Enhance disturbance rejection for open-loop unstable process with time delay. ISA Transactions 48, 237–244 (2009)
7. Rao, S., Chidambaram, M.: Enhanced two-degrees-of-freedom control strategy for second-order unstable processes with time delay. Ind. Eng. Chem. Res. 45, 3604–3614 (2006)
8. Padhy, P.K., Majhi, S.: IMC based PID controller for FOPDT stable and unstable processes. In: Proc. of 30th National System Conference, Dona Paula, Goa (2006)

Author Index

Printing: Mercedes-Druck, Berlin
Binding: Stein+Lehmann, Berlin